The Heart of a Man is a Woman

How to Find the One You've Always Wanted

Randall Curtis

Amrita Publications
San Anselmo, California
1995

The Heart of A Man Is a Woman. Copyright © 1995 by Randall Curtis. All rights reserved. No part of this book may be used or reproduced in any manner whatsoever without written permission from Amrita Publications except in the case of brief quotations embodied in critical articles and reviews.

First Edition
Printed in the United States of America

Publisher's Cataloging In Publication

Curtis, Randall, 1929-
   The heart of a man is a woman: how to find the one you've always wanted/Randall Curtis. -- 1st ed.
   p.cm.
   ISBN 0-9644459-6-4

   1. Astrology and sex. 2. Man-woman relationships I. Title.
BF1729.S4C87 1995   133.5'8'64677
                              QB194-21243

Amrita Publications
P.O. Box 2008
San Anselmo, CA 94979

Typesetting and Technical Support by Elizabeth Curtis
Cover Painting by Christa Marshall (see Appendix A-6)
Cover Design by Marianna Leuschel
Copy Editing by Genevieve Morgan

To my beloved Elizabeth; the one
I've always wanted

Special Thanks and Appreciation

To Elizabeth Curtis for her countless hours of typesetting and technical support. This book would not have been possible without her personal sacrifice in time and energy and "burning the midnight oil." Many thanks to Marianna Leuschel for her heartfelt support and creative gift in designing the cover of this book. A special appreciation and thanks to Christa Marshall for her permission to use her inspired painting for the cover. Many words of praise are due Genevieve Morgan for expert editing of the final draft. Finally, a million hugs to all my friends who shared the stories of their lives. Their troubles and triumphs transcend the written words of this book.

Contents

PART I THE HEART PROCESS

Chapter 1   THE AWFUL TRUTH AND THE WONDERFUL SECRET   1

Chapter 2   HOW TO AWAKEN THE LOVER IN YOUR HEART   11

The heart of you is love already • Only by losing your heart do you find it • Pursue who you love • The cell of fear • Be who you are • If you know who you are, you will find out what you want • Walking in and walking out • How not to get scarred

Chapter 3   HOW TO FIND THE ONE YOU'VE ALWAYS WANTED   27

The heart-awakened woman • The heart-awakened man • Summary

PART II PLANETARY CHEMISTRY

Chapter 4   WHAT IS PLANETARY CHEMISTRY?   37

Learning to live with the planets • Benefits others have enjoyed

Chapter 5   THE 12 ENERGY FIELDS OF THE SUN   47

Figure 1.

Chapter 6   THE IMPACT OF PLANETARY ENERGIES   59

The 12 energy fields of the Sun reveal our 12 basic attitudes

Chapter 7	THE FOUR PLANETARY EFFECTS	63
Chapter 8	THE FIVE PERSONAL PLANETS IN THE 12 ENERGY FIELDS	67

Example interpretation • Sun in the 12 energy fields - desire to survive • Moon and Venus • The Moon - desire for security • The Moon in the 12 energy fields • Venus - desire to receive love and to share feelings • Venus in the 12 energy fields • Mars - desire to take action • Mars in the 12 energy fields • Mercury - desire to think • Mercury in the 12 energy fields

Chapter 9	THE FIVE TRANSPERSONAL PLANETS AND THEIR EFFECTS	137

Jupiter - desire to acquire • Jupiter's positive and negative effects • Saturn - desire to separate • Saturn's positive and negative effects • Uranus - desire for independence • Uranus' positive and negative effects • Neptune - desire for ecstasy • Neptune's positive and negative effects • Pluto - desire of the soul • Pluto's positive and negative effects

Chapter 10	TABLE OF PERSONAL PLANETS	171
Chapter 11	THE PLUTONIAN PROCESS	173

Pluto as a visiting planet

Chapter 12	BASIC EFFECTS OF VISITING PLANETS	179

Table for visiting planets

Chapter 13	SCHEDULE OF VISITING PLANETS	189
Chapter 14	LISTENING TO THE VOICES OF THE PLANETS	199

An exercise with Saturn conjunct Venus • Chart A, Jana's childhood • Chart B, One man's emotional patterns

Chapter 15	READ THIS BEFORE GETTING MARRIED	211

Chart C, Brief portrait of a relationship

Chapter 16	THE MASTER TABLE	217
Chapter 17	HOW TO OBTAIN YOUR PLANETARY PATTERNS	221
	The easy way • The challenging way	
Appendix	FURTHER ADVENTURES IN PLANETARY CHEMISTRY	A-1

National Workshop Program

- Workshop A: Discover and Actualize What You Were Born To Do
- Workshop B: How To Find The One You've Always Wanted
- Workshop C: For Couples - Explore and Enhance Your Planetary Chemistry
- Workshop D: Do You Really Understand Your Child?
- Workshop E: Three Hour Workshop For You Alone
- Workshop F: How To Use The Planets For Every Day of Your Life
- Other Services: Personal Planetary Profiles, Insights For Therapists, Enhance Your Spiritual Practices, Planetary Journeys For Musicians And Other Artists, Business Plans and Career Moves, and Helpful Solutions For Everyday Problems

How to obtain prints of the cover painting	A-6
Order Form	A-7

Part I

The Heart Process

1

The Awful Truth and the Wonderful Secret

The Awful Truth

Death came into my life in August of 1985 and I have never been the same since. It was the death of who I thought I was as a man. I crashed heart-first into the awful truth and fell to pieces.

My crash into the awful truth cracked open my heart and forced all my feelings to the surface. I felt raw at the core. The search for love intensified and I became obsessed with women. Suddenly, in spite of the risk to my fragile ego, I fanatically pursued what I thought to be the answer to love. Whatever woman I was attracted to, I engaged her openly, foolishly, and with great intensity. All things feminine became a fascinating mystery to me. I hungered to know what love for a woman was really like.

Sometimes this hunger made me too open. I was willing to risk loss and rejection if it meant I would discover love. I walked into threatening places. They were frightening, thrilling, terrifying, but never boring. I lived on the edge of failure because I stuck my neck out first. I encountered each potential lover straight on with my heart right on my tongue, saying exactly how I felt. This scared some women away, but I had no patience for romantic games. The desire for truth was too intense.

A friend once told me that I should stop being so honest with women; that I would scare them away. He said, "You can't tell women how you feel about them like that. You only spook them." I said, "I know, but I can't help it. I don't have time to waste on games. I'm only interested in finding love. If they can't take the truth of my feelings, they are not for me anyway. I would rather know the truth and suffer the loss than to live a lie. It's the only way I know how to find out about love."

Some women seemed fascinated by my intense displays of affection for them. Some had a curious interest in the way I expressed my feelings, but others ran as fast as they could in the opposite direction. I felt I had to force love out into the open, away from the pretense and playing. I wanted to dance with love in front of me so that I could grasp the true essence of a woman. I wanted to know her and fully understand her. Even though there were many times when I fell on my face and understood nothing, I continued searching, following my feelings.

Women became a source of wonder. It was as if they possessed a magic secret that I could discover by chasing them with my heart. This inner compulsion propelled me toward the awful truth that revealed parts of myself I never knew.

I found that each woman reflected my inner feeling in some way and that I had to get to the bottom of that feeling. I soon saw that every woman I loved actually reflected a part of me. By knowing her emotionally and intimately, and by being totally open to her, she revealed to me a piece of myself. It was as if I gained from each of them a piece of my own heart that I had never known. This revelation inspired me and drove me onward. In some sense, I knew I was a fool for being so open about how I felt, but I was not going to hide anymore. I had done that all my life.

THE AWFUL TRUTH AND THE WONDERFUL SECRET

I was totally obsessed with knowing what love really was. I was after the truth even though I did not realize how awful it would be.

Every woman I was attracted to brought me closer to the awful truth. She drew me into a dark cave where I had no control. I did not know what was in there. I felt like I was entering a forbidden place, but I could not resist the journey. I had to know what was in there. I laid my heart out to them and some of them took it. I did not know if they would give it back or what they would do with it. I was totally absorbed in who they were and gave my innermost feelings to them. It seemed to me that they took these feelings into themselves, danced with them, laughed at them, and played with them as if they were a beach ball. Sometimes they would throw my heart back at me. I often sank, quietly trembling, fearing they were going to crush it and I would die. Still I could not resist telling them how much I loved them, no matter how carelessly they played with my feelings.

I was determined to follow wherever my feelings led me because I had always approached love with my mind and I got nowhere. I was never in touch with my feelings enough to know how I felt or who I was as a man. I was too scared of those feelings. In the past, whenever a woman asked me how I felt about something or someone, I would stare at her like a zombie and usually reply, "I'll have to think about that." At the time, my reply seemed very natural, but this kind of response is just as ridiculous as if you were to ask a person if they loved another person and they reply, "Well I think I do." I soon discovered that thinking had nothing to do with love. I intuitively felt that by engaging the woman I was attracted to with an open heart, with honesty, and with real feelings, I would eventually find the answer to love, itself. But I did not know how this answer would come about, and I knew nothing about the awful truth.

Women acted as unknowing guides or teachers who led me to the awful truth and finally to the wonderful secret. They did not seem to be aware of the deeper process they awakened within me. Perhaps it was because they were more engaged in dealing with my obsession or fascination for them. At the time of these intense encounters, I did not know that I was living out my illusions of the feminine. Because I was out of touch of any love for myself, I looked outside for love and support — for nurturing. I assumed in women qualities they did not actually have but only seemed to possess. The part of me that was missing (my feminine self, my inner lover) I saw outside of myself in the idealized form of one woman I was involved with: the one who would at last bring me the love I was seeking. In this regard, Silver was my greatest teacher.

Since I was not in touch with my inner woman (or what I consider my heart), Silver mirrored my feminine self. She became my ideal, or so I fully believed. But this was a romantic illusion in full bloom. It had nothing to do with real love. My "love" for her was destined to fail.

> *"A man without a soul, [heart] is but half a man, consequently when his soul is projected onto another human being it is as though half of himself were in her. The woman becomes enormously important as well as enormously attractive to him. He longs to get into relation with her, for by so doing he will come into relation once more with his own soul, which is otherwise lost to him."* (M. Esther Harding, *The Way of All Women*)

I felt I was this man without a soul because I gave the power of my illusions to Silver. She used this power to her own advantage, manipulating my emotions to get just about anything she wanted. She was in control of the cookie jar.

> *"Her natural capacity to attract the man's anima [soul - feminine illusion] gives her an importance and power which are in a certain sense fictitious, for she has done nothing to merit them. They depend solely on the man's illusion. It is like a fortune put into her hands for which she has not had to work. To sacrifice this power requires real devotion to a purpose or value which is superior to her own ego."* (M. Esther Harding, *The Way of All Women*)

I did not realize that Silver was the part of myself that I was trying to discover through becoming intimate with her. I thought she was my love, not an illusion of it. I had no idea that she was merely a reflection of my own illusions of a woman; that she was not who I thought she was. My short life with her ended in intense suffering. My illusions turned to disillusions. I became depressed at the core of my being. Life became the blackest cloud I had ever stumbled through. Was this the dark night of my soul? How could I go on? I asked myself, "Where is love?" The answer hit me like a falling rock. *Love is nowhere to be found in another. It is within you. It is not outside of your skin.*

Like Silver, each lover that took my heart, broke off a piece of it. They shattered my defenses and I was faced with my empty fantasies. This was the end of the illusion that I had always carried inside of me. I was confronted with the awful truth: *No one can ever give you the love you are looking for.* The search for that one perfect person who gives absolute love, freely without holding back, guaranteed forever, is fruitless. The awful truth is that this kind of love never happens; there is no such gift. No one can do this. Love has to be discovered inside of oneself.

In my own experience, I found women who would love me in small ways, but I could not find a woman who would awaken a source of love inside me by giving me love. My longing and need to be fulfilled by a woman had to be shattered. I realized that the looking and the seeking outside for love had to come to an end before I could find the real thing. When I realized that the love I was looking for was never going to come from the outside, hope evaporated and I emotionally died. Each woman that broke my heart gave me back the pieces. Each piece was an illusion that said: "I can't love you the way you want. I can't give you the love you are looking for. Your fascination with me is just an illusion. I am not who you think I am. You have to find that lover within yourself."

My belief that somewhere, someplace there would be a woman who would just love me, accept me totally for who I was and love me unconditionally, had to come to an end. I discovered that to know love, I had to be turned in upon my own heart without anything to lean on. In short, to know love, my heart had to be broken.

All of the women I knew during this time did break a part of me. Certainly none ever fulfilled me. How could they? They were the teachers of the awful truth. The awful truth that *no one was ever going to give me the love I was looking for* rang in my heart over and over again. Somehow I knew I had to find this love in my own soul, but I did not know how. I felt a barren emptiness without any inner sense of support. The awful truth became devastating. If love could not be found in another how would I ever find it within myself. I certainly did not feel it within me. I felt totally dead.

I was stuck with only an empty shell for a heart. The awful truth sank into my bones. I had to find love within myself? This seemed like an impossible task.

Finally, the first awakening of this love came to me in the form of a vision. It was a transforming psychic experience of my own heart as a man; it set me on the path to real love and the discovery of the wonderful secret.

THE AWFUL TRUTH AND THE WONDERFUL SECRET

The Wonderful Secret

On an ordinary sunny day in September, 1985, I had a remarkable vision that changed my life. This vision came in the midst of my fading illusions and near the end of my discovery of the awful truth.

I was sitting in my car under the shade of a tree waiting to see if Silver would come out of her office. I thought my heart would break. I felt like a thousand piano wires were squeezing it in two. Why did love hurt so much? How could one woman have so much control over my life? I was desperate for the answer.

It was all so one-sided. Silver had all the aces and I held the joker. I was suffering her continuous manipulation and rejection. She was on one of her "retreats" from me and I had not seen her for days. I didn't like being under her control, but she had my heart and I felt I could do nothing about it. I tried with every ounce of my desire to understand the suffering. I said to myself, "There must be an answer somewhere. I need that answer now. This pain is unbearable." I looked over at the office and saw Silver get in her car and drive away. My heart leaped. I drove after her. But when I caught up with her, it wasn't Silver at all. It was a woman who looked like her and who had the same kind of car. I was stunned. My desire made me a fool. I parked and went into a bookstore in search of an answer.

I bought a book entitled, *The I and the Not-I* by M. Esther Harding. I can't remember much about that book now, but I remember driving back to the shady tree and studying it. It touched a nerve. The writer talked a lot about the things that we are and the things that we are not. I was reading a passage where she wrote that a man will often see qualities in a woman that are not really there. Harding said a man projects his own inner woman (his feminine self) onto another woman because he does not understand his inner woman himself and that this kind of love is an illusion. Even though I had read this passage before in her other books, the meaning sank deeper into me this time. How could what I was feeling possibly be an illusion? If so, it was the most painful illusion I had ever created. I struggled to understand what this meant.

I stared at a woman walking down the street and began to compare her with Silver. "Why don't I feel as much for that woman on the street as I do for Silver?" I kept tracing my feelings back and forth between Silver and this stranger. I switched to another woman crossing in front of my car. I asked the same question and traced the feelings back and forth. "Why do I feel so much for Silver and nothing for this other woman? Why is this? Why do I feel so much pain for one woman and nothing for another? They are both women. What is the difference?" These were desperate and intense questions. I had to find the answer now, that very moment. Suddenly, I understood. There was no difference. I was making the difference. It was solely an act by myself. My own feelings were making the difference. Silver had nothing to do with it, except to trigger an illusion in me. In other words, I thought I was a victim of love rather than the one causing my suffering.

When I fully saw that I was the one who was making the difference and that Silver did not have any mysterious power or control of my heart, I had a vision of a woman soaring into me like a bird and coming to rest at the center of my heart. When this happened, all the tension in my body and the wires around my heart dissolved like ice in a hot sun. All the pain faded and washed away as I sat in wonder. The woman had come home. Home to my heart where she had always been. I saw that I, myself, was the love I was looking for. I had come home to embrace my own feminine. My own inner woman who had never revealed herself to me before. She was no longer separate from me. Although she had never been away, it truly felt like she had come home. I knew my own heart for the first time.

My heart was a woman! I had totally opened myself up to her by giving my heart to many women and she finally came back to me as one; the one I was looking for. The love I was looking for in Silver was already inside of me. Already there to nurture me. I did not need Silver to sustain my own feelings of love. I was love already, supported from within. Suddenly a new understanding flashed through me. I saw clearly that **the heart of a man is a woman and the heart of a woman is a man.** This was the wonderful secret revealed to me in my vision.

2

How to Awaken the Lover in Your Heart

The Heart of You Is Love Already

When you fall in love, where does this love come from? Where does it begin? If these questions puzzle you, try to feel them. Do you remember falling in love? Have you ever gazed into a stranger's eyes and experienced an overwhelming feeling in your heart? If so, that feeling arose from within you first. This stranger may have awakened this feeling, but love had to be inside of you for you to experience it; otherwise, it could not have happened. But why does this particular man do this to you? It is because he has a special chemistry that reflects and stimulates your heart, because your heart, as a woman, is a man.

As we have seen from my own experience, the woman did not pour love into me by some mysterious action. She simply awakened what was asleep. This means that love already exists inside of us. The true nature of our heart is love.

Obviously, love can come from the outside because someone can love us, but they cannot make us love ourselves. Without self love, all the love in the world from another person cannot make us feel whole. But we cannot simply decide to feel love for ourselves. It will not work. Something has to happen to us. There has to be a "change of heart." Strange as it may sound, this love and respect for ourselves begins to awaken when we truly lose our hearts to another.

Only By Losing Your Heart Do You Find It

When you give your heart to another, you lose it. You cannot take it back. Why should you protect yourself from a broken heart? Most of us spend too much energy trying to keep from being hurt when a broken heart may be exactly what we need. At least we would be alive, feeling, vulnerable, and capable of feeling compassion for others.

If you engage a man with an open heart you will begin to process the pain of resistance locked in your body. You will allow yourself to feel the pain, know it, and fully engage your attraction with open eyes filled with courage and adventure. This is the greatest cure for a loveless heart and it will bring you to your true power as a woman. This moment of love is a gift. Even if it fails, you will win in the end. You will discover your true strength as a woman, make peace with your inner male, and discover him as yourself. You will come to know true intimacy.

The fire of love burns away the fear of intimacy. When a man awakens your heart, he may truly reflect it or he may reflect only your illusion of love. But how will you know him unless you engage him emotionally and intimately? In real love, you have no defense. You have no choice but to feel it. You lose it. You lead with your feelings, get your heart swept away, and become transformed in the process. This is the wonderful secret of love. The way to your own heart-power. You cross the bridge of no return by completely giving your heart to the man who awakens your feelings. There is nothing you can do about it. Nothing else will seem true. This is the point of no return. You make the journey.

If your journey is not clear, free, and open, you will tend to project the nature of your love upon a man or fall in love with an illusion of yourself and attract those men who reflect your own problems about love, e.g., fear of commitment, reluctance to feelings of vulnerability, and conflicts between freedom and attachment. Or perhaps you are attracted to relationships, wherein you choose (perhaps unconsciously) to be the victim, suffering abuse and rejection because you may have had a similar relationship with your father. If you resist losing your heart to the man who has awakened it — illusion or not — you will prevent the mysterious process that will bring you to a new self-awareness and a profound sense of self-respect and genuine self-caring. Your illusions about men can be broken if you engage them fully and process the pain locked inside of you.

But the only man you can fully engage emotionally is the one that **you** love. Otherwise, you will not risk rejection and stay vulnerable long enough to understand your relationship to him. But it is absolutely necessary to take this leap. *Only by losing your heart, do you find it.* If you give your heart away, it will come back to you in the form of new strength and wholeness. You cannot know your heart until you have given it away. In order to find your heart, you have to give it to your lover first without knowing that your love will ever be returned. This takes great courage, a willingness to leap into the fire of a relationship instead of dancing on the edge where cowards ponder the mystery of love.

Everything is mysterious and uncertain when we give our heart to another. But we are foolish to hold back and protect ourselves from rejection. We may very well get burned. That's the chance we need to take, and even if we do get "mooshed" (as my beloved wife, Elizabeth, calls it), we will find a treasure we never thought we possessed. A chunk of our own power is released and awakened within us. A heart full of love, strong and certain, is born out of intense relationships. Not just "OK" ones. Knowing this, we must courageously engage relationships from the heart and put an end to those useless and mediocre encounters that take us nowhere or lead us into miserable marriages that entangle us in a web of senseless karma.

If you have never given your heart away, you are missing love's greatest gift. Are you waiting to be loved or will you risk being the first to love? Why not become a lover by pursuing and engaging the adventures of love and relationships until the man in your heart is awakened.

Pursue Who You Love

Instead of waiting to find a man to love you, look for the man you can love. This will help awaken the man in your heart. If you only have a relationship where the man loves you more than you love him you will always be in control. You are not in a position to be vulnerable or to grow in power and self-respect. Being in control is not about being in love. It is about living in fear of losing your heart. While it is comfortable and safe to have someone love you, you are denying yourself a chance to discover your own heart and its mysterious power. You will not know your heart by playing it safe and choosing those relationships that are predictable and emotionally dead. You may even attract those men who are not good for you. They will not require that you give your heart because they live in terror of surrendering their own. But if you don't really care for someone, you don't have much of a chance for true intimacy in that relationship. And, as true lovers know, intimacy is not just going to bed with someone. Intimacy is sharing your inside self with your lover without fear, disguise, or pretense. It is letting yourself be known just as you are from the inside and opening wide the door to your heart.

The Cell of Fear

Many people refuse to open their heart's door and let themselves be known. Their feelings are locked up in a cell of fear. There is a sign on the cell door which says, "Do Not Enter." They are terrified of intimacy. True intimacy is avoided as if it was a disease. Some are still living out patterns that may reach beyond this lifetime. It would be death to give their heart away. Though they may not know it, living in this cell is actually more painful than opening up because their own self-nurturing power is cut off. Their fear prevents them from knowing their own goodness. Their heart is in jail.

When love is stirred in the heart, it usually arouses a deep-seated fear of love itself. It is this resistance, sealed in the very cells of our bodies, that seems to remember our childhood suffering. That's why we say, "Love hurts." The radiant power of the heart itself is pushing against this pain, shaking the cell door.

Real love is not merely a cupid's arrow, a lighthearted romance. It is a sword of fire that burns through us, opens us up, makes us feel raw and defenseless. We try to prevent this transformation because it hurts so much. But in order to really love, our heart has to be broken. It is this wall of defense that gets shattered. Keeping this door closed is what most people do all of their lives. But if we want to know real love, we have to swing the door wide open and surrender our heart to feeling. When we do this, our own goodness pours out of us. This heart-power sustains us when we need help. It is not poured into us by another. It is love itself radiating through us. For a woman, this is when the man has come home. He is awake and free inside of her. She is no longer at war with him because she discovers him as her self. The source of her own power. She knows who she is because she knows who the man is.

Be Who You Are

If a man does not like you the way you are, then he is not yours. It is a mistake to try and change ourselves for another person. We all have faults, but if we try to be something we are not, we will be miserable. If we do not have a great deal of self-respect for ourselves, we will lose what little we do have if we stay with a person who is always pointing out the ways do not measure up. As the well-known Gestalt therapist, Fritz Perls, said, "We are not here to live up to other people's expectations." Besides, this kind of demand has nothing to do with love. It shows that this person does not like us the way we are. They don't really know us and probably think we are someone we are not.

If You Know Who You Are, You Will Find Out What You Want

We owe it to ourselves to discover who we are and what we desire in another person so we do not give them a false impression of who we are. This will not happen if we are clear in our feelings about ourselves. Remember what Shakespeare said, "To thine own self be true, and as night follows day, you cannot be false to any man (or woman)." But in order to be true to our own self, we must feel and know who that self really is.

Many women complain that they can't get men to talk about their feelings. The truth is that most men do not know how they feel. They do not know who they are emotionally and therefore cannot be true to a self that is hidden behind a mask of pretending. One young lady complained to her father that he never seemed to care or talk about his feelings for her. He replied by saying, "Well, I take you out to dinner and buy you clothes and things. Doesn't that show you that I love you?" A father may not have any idea how to express love for his daughter. He may have trained himself to suppress his feelings since childhood and as an adult he is not in touch with them. It is natural for him to be terrified of exploring how he truly feels. He has not yet learned to honor his emotions and to respect them. But as long as he is locked into a defensive strategy, he cannot know who he really is as a man.

If we do not know our heart, our true feelings, and live inspired by our fantasies and dreams, we will be false to others. We will not live and act according to our true nature. We will live, hiding behind our masks, and people will tend to misunderstand us. Perhaps this was what the actress, Melanie Griffith, meant when she described her troubled marriage:

> *"What's sad is that you have a dream of being with a person and you want to fit them into your dream, and they have a dream of you, and they want to fit you into their dream, <u>but it's not who you both really are.</u>"* (Liz Smith, *San Francisco Chronicle*, 8/2/94)

If we do not know who we really are, we will choose those people who respond to a self that is not who we are. If we have a deep fear of exposure, we will live false lives and cannot be true to the one we have chosen. In truth, if we do not know ourselves, we reveal only our mask to our lover and they mistake this mask for who we are. Our lover cannot honor who we are if we do not know our own feelings — if we are out of touch with them. This is why we need to pursue that which we love and not wait to be loved. If we lead with our heart, make ourselves open and vulnerable, our mask falls away and we discover our true feelings.

Many of us have denied our own feelings since childhood because someone in charge squashed them, repressed them, or did not honor them. We did not have a chance to discover our own depths. We were trained not to honor our feelings, or respect or discover who we were. Many of us even practiced trying to be invisible to avoid being seen by our tormentors. This repression made us feel worthless because good things did not come to us. We faced cruelty, criticism, and denial. Since good things like praise, support, and success were never ours, we assumed that we did not deserve them. Now, as an adult, we sense that we are unworthy and not important. We feel unhappy about who we are and do not know how to find our own value because it seems cut off from us. But no matter how difficult it is, we must recapture our capacity to feel and recognize our own goodness. We must allow space to really know what our feelings are. Our passion will never be aroused if we have not discovered how it feels to know who we really are. We cannot know what we want if we don't know how we feel. Obviously, this can be very difficult. It is not easy to free ourselves from a suppressed childhood of negative experiences.

As a child, I was beaten by my father with a razor strap and birch switches. My mother beat me with curtain rods. Imagine what this did for my self-worth! I mention this because it took me most of my life to recognize my own goodness. This discovery of self-worth occurred by giving my whole heart to each lover. I knew no amount of therapy or positive thinking can ever be as effective as opening our heart to those whom we love or even think we love, because that very act of opening has the power to awaken us to our own self-respect. Here is what one of my clients said about this process:

> *"I finally listened to your suggestion which was to allow myself to fall in love. Not only did I experience my capacity to love deeply but I experienced a depth of pain so much at my core that I seemed immobilized for a time. But, oh, what a teaching I have had and what a wondrous gift I was given –*

> *— for I know myself now in a way that I was unconscious to prior to meeting the man I fell in love with."*

Without this deep sense of goodness, we cannot accomplish great things. If we do not know what we want, it is because we have not allowed ourselves to feel who we really are. We must first process the pain that is preventing us from being truly intimate with others and with ourselves. However, it is very difficult for a man or woman to surrender their heart or process the pain of childhood when they have been so abused.

I personally know hundreds of women who have been abused by men in their childhood. It is no wonder that they are angry and reluctant to give their hearts away to men. With such traumatic past experiences, it is quite natural for a woman to hold back and to respond in this way. But who is going to teach men the way, if not her? Her nurturing power is our only hope. She has the instincts to awaken a man into feeling and to teach him what love is, but she must be fully awakened into love herself. Of course, it is also the responsibility of men, but I am afraid they are not going to do it. They may be too motivated by fear to give up their control.

Likewise, a woman will not discover her heart-power by identifying with the masculine tendencies of control, logic, and materialism. Her heart and feeling must be brought back to nurture the earth. The paradox is that a woman's power as a woman and as a nurturing presence in the world can only emerge if she makes peace with the man in her heart. This does not make her more of a man. It frees her feminine power because she is no longer battling defensively with the male. When she has found her male self (her heart), she will function supremely well as a truly feminine woman with great wisdom, intelligence, and healing energy. She will be able to "compete" with men in the marketplace not by suppressing her nurturing energy, but by releasing it through a heart that no longer struggles with men emotionally. When she is awake to who she really is, feeling her male force inside, she will be free to be a true woman on the outside. It is this kind of woman who will bring the world back to the heart and to feeling.

When we come home to our heart through the love process described in this book, we will know who we are and what we want. When we know what we want, we will have the power to attract the one we have always wanted and walk away from those relationships that we do not want.

Walking In and Walking Out

If a relationship is not working, is not what you want, find a way to bring it to an end. Look for the warning signs, the red flag signals. Here are a few:

- **"It's your job to handle the finances. I don't have time for it."** The key control words are "it's your job" because a man is placing a condition upon you that you are supposed to follow. These are not cherishing signs. A more loving man might ask, "Do you want to handle the finances? I'm willing to do it, but I don't have much time," or "Would you like for me to handle the finances, or would you rather have separate accounts and just share expenses?" The point is that the loving mate is considerate and provides options. Making demands and dictating "shoulds" are signs of control and control is not about love. It is about fear. This is a strong red flag.
- **"You should be doing exercises every day so you can keep your weight down."** Be very wary when your potential partner uses this kind of should. This is a sure sign of control and manipulation. Love is not at the center of his intentions. You can be certain he has not given his heart to you because he does not like you the way

you are. Maybe you are overweight, but if he loved you, he would not put it to you that way. He simply would not express it in that manner.

- **"You're going out with them and leaving me here alone?"** This maneuver is very manipulative. You are supposed to feel guilty for going out, even when you mentioned it a week ago. If this man loved you, he would hope that you have a good time and be prepared to do his own thing that evening.

If there are signs of control and manipulation in your relationship, you are already living under a red flag. You may have to eventually walk away from this man, especially if you are growing and changing at the heart.

Why should you stay or be with someone whose energies do not harmonize with yours? Of course, it is difficult to walk away when you care for someone and are deeply involved with them. It is important to give it your best, so that you know you really tried in your heart. But you also have to care for yourself. You deserve to be loved and don't deserve to be abused. I remember the day I learned this powerful lesson.

In earlier days when I was still stumbling through my romantic illusions, I went after whatever woman I was attracted to. I knew I had to follow my impulses even if they led me into some strange places. I even knew I was chasing women who were no good for me but I felt the attraction was something I had to pursue and understand. I saw that if a woman had the power to attract me to her, she had something of value to teach me about love. Even though my emotions made a fool of me, I followed them anyway. Never before had I allowed myself to feel so much. The adventures were stimulating but also very painful. At times, I suffered intense rejections. But there was one rejection that set me off in a new direction. It was a gift. A remarkable discovery.

I was intensely attracted to a young woman (I will call her Diana) who was not attracted to me. It was a one-sided relationship from the start. She was dark, mysterious, and delicious to me. I really wanted her, but I saw that nothing was going to happen. She told me straight out that she liked me but didn't love me, but that we could still go to dinners and movies. It was a no-touch situation. I couldn't sleep. I got up and wrote her a letter and told her how much I loved her. When I finished the letter, I saw the painful road ahead: She was going to string me along and I was going to chase her. I could not bear the pain of being with her without being intimate with her. An idea flashed inside of me that told me I didn't have to suffer this kind of treatment anymore. I saw for the first time that I was better than that. I was worth being loved and didn't have to be with women who rejected me. I realized that I was not helpless. I could do something about it. I was struck with the realization that I was a good person and deserved to be loved. I never understood that before. I usually gave in to what women wanted but gave no power to what I really wanted. My heart lit up: "Why should I be with someone who doesn't love me? I'm worth more than that." This was not just an idea. It was a moving force that burned through my feelings and turned me around.

    When morning came, I called Diana and told her I had to see her right away, just for a minute. She said she had to go to work in twenty minutes. I said I would be there in five. When she answered the door, I walked inside, handed her the letter I had written and sat down. I said, "Everything I have been feeling about you is in this letter, but I wanted to tell you in person because I can't wait another day. I love you, but I know you don't love me. That's all right. It's not your problem. It's mine. But I can't stand being with you without being closer. I can't be with you or see you anymore. It's killing me." She said, "I really do care for you, and I have a lot of respect for you. It took a lot of courage for you to come here and tell me this." I said, "Maybe down the road we can be friends, but I can't be with you now. I have to say goodbye." She hugged me and kissed me. I walked out with tears running down my face.

As I walked to my car, something remarkable happened. I felt a surge of peace come over me. Suddenly, I felt clean, clear, real, and strong. How could I be feeling this way when I just told the girl I loved goodbye? I thought I would be totally devastated after letting her go. Instead, a feeling of new strength and happiness came over me. I felt like my own heart had become free by letting go of the very thing I loved. At last, I had taken a stand for who I was. I set myself free. Once again, my inner woman revealed that she was me. That I would always be sustained by her (my own heart). That I would never again be abandoned or feel that I was without love if a woman rejected me.

As you can see, in the process of having our heart broken, we do not have to endure abuse. If our present lover does not love us, we can walk away no matter how much it hurts. When we do this, we take a stand for our own goodness. Self-respect and self-value emerge. Live by giving your heart away. Chase that man who stirs you emotionally, but if he doesn't return your love after you have given him your best, don't hang around to try and convince him. Remember, if you have to fix it up, it will be wrong from the start. Be willing to say goodbye. Generate the courage to walk away. You will discover new strength, more self-caring, increased heart-energy, and you will not be scarred by the experience.

How Not to Get Scarred

You can be wounded deeply by a love experience, but if you release that wound from your heart you will not be scarred. If you do not practice releasing the lover who has wounded you, you will remain bitter and very reluctant to engage in new love experiences.

A friend of mine did not want to say that she still loved two men who rejected her because she was too proud, resentful, and angry with them. To admit her love for them was like saying "they got me." I pointed out that she still loved them in spite of what happened and that she would not be free of the anger and the hurt until she accepted her love for them. For a long time, she would not admit this. But finally she said, "You're right. I do still love them in spite of what they did to me."

How do you release someone who does not love you? In my own case, I realized that Diana did not belong with me because she did not recognize me as her lover. (By "belong," I do not mean my possession because we can never truly possess anyone.) She was not touched at the heart by who I was as a man. I saw this truly, and was not willing to chase a fantasy that had no hope of being realized. No matter how much it hurt, I knew I had to release her. I did this by letting her know all my feelings for her and why I was saying goodbye. I revealed myself to her. I let her know that I loved her. There was nothing left to hide or work out.

By releasing those who do not "belong" with us, we forgive them for rejecting us and thank them for awakening our heart; for making it possible to love more deeply the next time. There are millions of people in the world who are not meant to be with us. They are not ours to love and to be with. Some of our lovers will wound us deeply. Others will quickly come and go. But we must always release those who do not belong with us so that we will not become scarred and afraid to engage our future lover with even greater intimacy. The one we have always wanted is somewhere in the future or maybe in the present unrecognized. The more we engage in relationships from the heart and release those that are not ours, the sooner we create room in our heart to attract the one we have always wanted.

Attracting the one into your life that you have always wanted is a mysterious process. Your mate could be a very ordinary person to others, but very special to you. He will have what you like. He will fit inside your skin and you will love him just as he is. He will fill up your empty spaces, nurture you, cherish you and support you emotionally. He will accept your faults and bring you humor. He will enjoy you just as you are. You will not even think of changing him because he will reflect your heart. He will be your heart. You will not be concerned with who is in charge or who is the boss. It will never occur to you. You will rest in your feminine nature and he will rest in his masculine. Each of you will rest in your own goodness and share all of that with each other.

This is certainly my life with my wife, my beloved Elizabeth. She is my heart. A true reflection of my own feminine nature. Sometimes, when I look at her, I feel like I am fourteen again. Joy leaps out of me and I embrace her with wild abandon. The happiness is sometimes indescribable. Is she pouring love into me and making me happy? It is a mystery. I feel happy already. Her very presence triggers my heart and love pours out of me. She shows me who I am and what my feelings are. I feel like a heart-awakened man.

3

How to Find The One You've Always Wanted

As we have seen, there are two ways to attract the one you have always wanted: (1) *always remain vulnerable and (2) pursue that which moves you emotionally.* These attitudes process relationships quickly and remove obstructions to intimacy. When your internal reluctance to true intimacy has been broken, your heart vibrates at a higher frequency and you begin to attract men who are closer to the one you have always wanted. This is because you will be clearer and stronger. These new men begin to reflect your own love that you feel for yourself. They are closer to reflecting who you really are inside or who you arc becoming in your heart. This is the mysterious process of the magnetic power of the love-awakened heart: a vulnerable wound open to infinity.

The Heart-Awakened Woman

A woman who is vulnerable is living in a wound. She has already suffered the loss of control and defense against being hurt. She has awakened to a deeper intensity of feeling. If she lives in this wound long enough, she will learn that she is worth being loved. She begins to feel that any man who rejects her does not belong with her. She practices letting him go. She learns to truly release him, no matter how much pain she may feel in doing so. This practice of release opens her heart even more to herself and she begins to feel herself as a good and valuable person, worthy of love, respect, and the abundant things in life.

This woman discovers a great secret, a paradox: She does not have to struggle to awaken her feminine power. Her power naturally emerges as she fully embraces the male within her. By opening her heart completely to him, she discovers her own inner strength and finally comes to rest fully in her feminine nature.

At first, it does not feel like she is getting stronger—but she is. When she finally finds that self-nurturing place within her feelings, she is reborn. Men treat her very differently. Opportunities are laid at her feet and men of greater character, strength, and substance are drawn into her life. These men will be very different from the men she knew in the past before her transition. They will not be afraid to love. Since she is now clear in her heart and knows who she is, she attracts men who reflect her new clarity. More and more they come closer to her true ideal. Somewhere among these few men she will find her true mate — the one she has always wanted. It is inevitable. She may even recognize him immediately, as if she had known him for centuries, and now in this moment he is returning to finish the dinner they were having five hundred years ago. Sometimes it will feel just like that. She may have seen him years ago, but he passed in the night because she did not recognize him. Now he returns to be with her because she has made a place for him in her heart.

I had known my wife, Elizabeth, for two years before I "recognized" her. I was too busy chasing my romantic illusions to see through my own confusion. I did not know who she was because I did not know my own heart. One day, near the pinnacle of my process, she said "Hello" and my heart expanded. All of a sudden I found her very attractive. This was a strange and wonderful feeling because I had never felt that way about her before. It was as if I had seen her for the first time. A bell went off inside of me. When I awoke the next day, after our first evening together, I felt her intense presence inside of my body. My logical, male mind could not believe it. It was like a loving spirit bathing me in absolute bliss. In that instant I recognized her. I knew who she was. She was my heart. My true feminine spirit reflected in the outside world in her physical form. I have loved her intensely ever since.

The heart-awakened woman will know when she has come home. Home to her own heart and to her lifelong lover. She is not confused by fear or doubt anymore. Her heart and mind are clear. Because her heart is open, she lives by wisdom and understanding. She has something of great value to lean on and to refer back to — her own heart-power. She is a heart-awakened woman.

This heart-awakened woman already has love to give. She is radiant with self-respect and self-caring. She has already made the journey from self-hate to real self-love. She has paid the price of discovery. She has survived a rite of passage wherein she endured the heart's great fire while it consumed her reluctance to surrender to a lover. Now, she will not tolerate a man who has no capacity to love her. She will walk away. She does not give as an act of sacrifice. Her giving is spontaneous. She can truly help herself and others because she is sustained by the power of her own love-awakened heart. She has love to give abundantly.

She is a real lover who does not sacrifice herself out of need for love but because it is a gift of her own love felt inside that radiates outward. Love is already flowing from her. She gives because it is the nature of love itself. She does not give out of a need to get love. She is love already. But she did not reach this fullness within herself without enduring the heart's great journey. She knows and understands the heart's intense fire. She has learned to live in the "wound." She is a woman who is willing to take the journey and live through a period of extreme vulnerability. She has lived her own death.

There was a time when this woman felt that she was doing all the loving and getting nothing back; that she was the one who was always reaching out while others seemed to turn away. For a long time, she felt the wound in her heart would never heal. Love from another did not seem to exist. It was nowhere to be found. Despair engulfed her being and she did not know where to turn. She was forced in upon herself and became weary from trying to stop the pain. She tried everything to stop from feeling so intensely — to distract herself from the suffering. She escaped into movies, ate too much too often, pretended to enjoy the company of boring and shallow people, worked on projects like a zombie, or tried to return to an old relationship that would not require any risk.

She experienced the profound meaning of the awful truth and the great disappointment. Her romantic bubble broke open and evaporated. At times, she endured deep depressions because all illusions about love were gone. She felt there was no love anywhere. She saw that no one was or could give her the love she wanted. It was a shattering discovery. Men had to fail her in order for her to confront this awful truth. To shatter the illusions of her romantic projections.

Then came the birth of a new truth about relationships. There was not one shred of tolerance for playing games to get what she wanted. There emerged a new clarity in her heart and feelings. She became open and clear. She knew what kind of man she wanted, but she no longer looked for him out of need. Love flowed freely out of her but there was not yet anyone who could receive it. At last, she was ready to give love without seeking it.

The heart-awakened woman finds the man she has always wanted not by a conscious choice, but by the mysterious attraction of her heart already fully opened into radiance by love itself.

The Heart-Awakened Man

The journey of the heart-awakened man is hardly different from that of the woman. I have revealed my own struggles in this journey with the hope that other men will confront their own death and discover their remarkable feminine self.

For a man to discover his strength, he does not have to try to be a man by performing great physical or mental feats. Many men suffer from the misconception that this is the way to their power. A man has to engage the feminine to find his power, not the masculine. He is already male. Even though his male side may also be wounded, it is far more beneficial for him to *learn to feel* first. Then he has an emotional connection to his own heart. A man needs to embrace this feeling self which is the true source of wisdom, nurturing and support.

Robert Bly, a poet who is very active in the men's movement, says that men must break away from the "mother" to develop emotionally. Other authorities argue that this break can create a sense of alienation from the mother and foster hostility toward women. This book offers a different approach based on the heart's natural wisdom.

A man, upon entering a love relationship, must engage his mother figure, eventually transcending his need to be nurtured and sustained by a woman emotionally while remaining in relationship with her. He cannot do this by avoiding intimacy with her. He must confront the truth of his childish needs. A cold and unloving mother can make this very difficult for a man because he will avoid true intimacy with other women and become terrified of their rejection. Although he may run from rejection, he will only back into it. No woman can give him the love he needs; and a mature woman will refuse to play the mother role with him. He will not be successful at undoing his emotional dependency on the woman if he abandons or ignores trying to establish a truly intimate relationship with her and resorts to being a mere macho man in the world.

It is true that a man has to break away from the mother to develop emotionally, but this weaning must come from discovering his own inner mother while engaged with a woman intimately from the heart. He stays in this fire until the transformation is complete. He cannot do this by separating from women and denouncing the mother.

Men can teach other men how to develop their will and how to be strong in the world. They can also express great love for each other, but they cannot teach each other about the feminine. Bonding with other men can be very positive and energizing but if a man does not understand the feminine, he does not understand himself. A man is not just a man; he is also a woman — but men seem to know so little about their inner feminine. This is quite strange when we think about it. He grew in a woman's body for nine months, lived off her food, her energy and her breath. He even went to bed with her for nine months! How close can he get? Yet men are still puzzled over the feminine psyche and are terrified of having an intimate connection with her.

A man's feeling nature is the woman in his heart. If he is afraid of her and strategically avoids or suppresses his feelings, he will function like a zombie, just as I did. Only part of him will be alive. He will not know how he really feels about anything and therefore will have no wisdom in the world. To really know his heart and to experience his power, a man must become very vulnerable to the woman so that she can teach him who she is. He will then learn who he is emotionally. This process requires that he surrender his heart to her in spite of his inner terror. His heart of stone and his emotional dependency on the woman for nurturing must be broken. He must continue to lead with his feelings until his defenses against love are dissolved. When this happens, he will stand forth as a true man, strong and capable of giving his heart and life to his lover. He will no longer be afraid of a woman and her feelings. He will understand her at last. He will become more of a man by embracing his feminine self. This does not mean that he will become more like a woman. He will be more of a man because he will no longer be afraid of the mother's control, the manipulation of the witch, or the guiles of the bitch — all parts of himself. He will simply understand them all because he has confronted them within himself. This is the heart-awakened man.

Summary

- Look at a love relationship as a way to open your heart, because only an open heart will have the power to attract the one it has always wanted. If you have never given your heart away, how could you know love? All other affairs are simply rehearsals for the real thing.
- The quality of those people you attract will improve as the quality of your loving improves because you will learn how to release those people who do not belong with you and who do not reflect your heart.
- Go after the person you love. Do not wait for them to come to you. You will lose control, not be able to play it safe, nor able to manipulate the relationship. Your mask of self-defense will fall away and you will discover your own depths. This is your true empowerment as a woman.
- You must put yourself in a vulnerable position that exposes your true feelings. These are raw and terrifying feelings which begin a process that may be repeated

because your first lover — the first one you actually give your heart to — will rarely be the one you have always wanted nor yours to be with, although you may think so. He is usually there to teach you what it feels like to give your heart away and not be able to get it back! When you have known this feeling, you will cross the bridge of no return. You will not retreat because it hurts. You will break the cycle of self-protection against love and you will begin the wonderful process that will bring you home to your heart.

When you have completed your process by knowing the awful truth, you will awaken to an overflowing feeling in your heart. You will be love itself, know your own power, and know who you are as a woman.

I was compelled to go through this process, but you can duplicate it by an act of will. You don't have to wait for it to happen to you. The new world you are about to enter will give you many tools to help you do this and help you find your way to the one you have always wanted.

Part II

Planetary Chemistry

4

The Secret Chemistry of Relationships

When I first began my adventure with the planets thirty-five years ago, I was constantly amazed by what I discovered. I could not believe such ideas had always been available. I was so awed by the accuracy and depth of the insights that I often stayed up until sunrise digging out the nuggets imbedded in the mystery of the planets.

Now you can use this ancient wisdom to fully understand yourself and all of your relationships. To succeed in your journey, all you need is a desire to leap beyond your ordinary perceptions and release your mind into the mysterious world of planetary chemistry and its remarkable secrets. Complete this journey, and you will emerge with a new vision for looking into the hearts of others.

Although there are many self-help movements that try to teach us how to repair relationships, few of them provide a method for discovering whether another person's energies are in harmony with ours at the beginning of the relationship. In this section, you will discover some amazing secrets about your lover's energy and be able to determine if that energy is in harmony with yours. What you are about to learn will give you some remarkable tools that you will be able to use for the rest of your life.

Learning to Live With The Planets

Many years ago, I ran into a woman friend in a restaurant who introduced me to a lady who was with her. (I will call that lady Stranger.) The moment we sat down, I felt an intense energy run through my body. My stomach jumped around and I couldn't take my eyes off of Stranger. Within five minutes or less, I was holding her hand. Even though we both were thoroughly embarrassed, I could not resist pursuing her affections. I was overcome with desire and I knew she was, too. I asked her out for dinner and she accepted. We had many romantic evenings, but we eventually parted. Other elements of our lives did not fit — but the passion was overwhelming.

What was this energy? Most of us would say "chemistry" and let it go at that. But after studying the heavens for thirty-five years, I knew the answer was created by the special chemistry of our planets. It was our unique planetary chemistry. Her Uranus at birth was in the solar field of Taurus in conjunction with my Venus in Taurus at birth. I know. You're wondering "What on earth is he talking about?" Let me explain this by referring you to the energy wheels of the body or "chakras."

According to the ancient yogis, the chakras are seven subtle nerve centers that run along the spine. Each center is ruled by a planet. Our major sexual center is the second nerve center up from the base of the spine. This center is ruled by the planet Venus. The planet Uranus rules the pituitary gland which regulates sexuality. When I came into contact with Stranger, her Uranus energy in Taurus in a sense ignited and intensified my sexual center (Venus in Taurus) which sparked an irresistible desire. This contact also seemed to lift her into an exalted state of passion because my Venus center stimulated her higher Uranus center of feeling and awareness. Basically what this contact amounted to was a transcendental form of sexual energy between us which I had never experienced before. It was very hard to let her go. It could have easily turned into an obsession, but because we lived different lives, we had to say goodbye. That was a very difficult thing to do because we were addicted to the energy that was generated between us.

It is not important whether or not you believe or disbelieve that other people can spin your chakras. But it is obvious to me that when two people are attracted to each other, there is an energy exchange between them. This energy travels through space. Perhaps you have had a similar experience of obsession, but you may have never thought of that energy as having anything to do with the planets or other people spinning your chakras.

Think of this energy as planetary chemistry, a unique energy field set up by the planets and the patterns they form at the time of our birth. There is a simple way to actually unravel the mystery of this energy by understanding how our own planetary birth patterns relate to the planetary birth patterns of another person. Even though the planets create fixed patterns in our nature at birth, they continue to move and act upon our original patterns. Other people's energies also affect our fixed planetary birth patterns. Always keep in mind that these birth planets are different parts of yourself. By exploring their subtle, psychic relationships, you will discover who you are and transcend the limitations of science.

Most scientists see nothing subtle about the planets. It seems that they consider them nothing more than celestial bodies for material study. When pieces of the Comet Shoemaker-Levy 9 exploded on Jupiter in July 1994, astronomers had a field day observing the cosmic explosions. They were totally absorbed and intrigued by the new physical discoveries they were making, but few have given much thought to the psychic or psychological effects the planets represent. This is like looking at an intricately designed machine, taking it apart and analyzing its pieces, but never turning it on to see how it really functions. I suppose they are involved in rocks, ices and gases because they have no model for exploring the psychic effects of planets. These psychic effects have been apparent to countless mystics through the centuries. It is fortunate that we do not need to wait for scientific research or sanction to eventually determine that there are more to the planets than material substances. We can make our own psychological discoveries overnight. Besides, the planetary chemistry between people, human events, and relationships is a mystery that may never be understood or fit into a scientific model. It is so vast and yet incredibly intricate in detail. However this need not prevent us from reaping the rewards by studying the meaning of the planets and their intimate, esoteric connection to us.

We are not just earth beings. We are also heaven-born. Even though we are incarnate on earth, there is no "down here." We were also born in the sky simultaneously. The sky is the home of the earth. It is everywhere around us. Like the earth, the other planets are wandering spaceships. But the planets are more than our companion travelers. They are not just physical objects stuck "out there" to entertain astronomers. They are part of us. They tell us who we are in the greatest detail. We are closely linked to their psychic energies because we are intimately involved in their evolution. (Their physical distance from us appears to have nothing to do with it. They affect the psychic dimension which is not limited by time and space.) The patterns they form together are full of meaning and the way in which they relate to each other at the time of our birth shows us who we are. They form a celestial chemistry that is expressed in our human chemistry. This is a startling idea, but it is absolutely true. I do not know why the planets relate so intimately with us, but they do. Certainly we could spend lifetimes trying to find out why, but this is not necessary. The planets' patterns offer us a boundless source of knowledge when we calculate the time, date, and place of birth of any person or event. We can learn to use this knowledge for every day of our lives.

You will soon learn how to analyze your own birth patterns and understand your relationship to other people. We will take one step at a time. If you are patient, you will emerge with many refreshing and rewarding insights into the hearts and minds of others. You will also be able to use this new awareness to focus your life in the direction you should be going according to the messages revealed in your birth patterns. There is nothing mystical in this process. It is a very useful practice which you will soon enjoy.

It was very useful for me to know that Stranger's Uranus in Taurus was near the same place in the heavens as my Venus in Taurus. This planetary, energy connection explained why we were so attracted to each other physically. Yet the rest of our planetary patterns were out of sync. We did not have much in common in other areas. Even though we enjoyed each other immensely in a physical sense, we knew the rest of us would not work well together. This was completely confirmed by a closer look at our other planets and how they related to each other.

Any relationship between two people can be thoroughly explained by the planetary patterns they form together without the interpreter even knowing or seeing them personally. This in itself is remarkable. I have analyzed the relationship of many couples whom I have never met. Many sessions were done over the phone at long distances. They were amazed at how much the planets revealed about them and whether they could make it together. This information gave them a profound understanding of each other and the insights they needed to make a decision. Some of them were married. Others said goodbye.

Aside from the Sun and Moon, the planets are hardly noticed by most of us, even though they have been with us for eons. They travel across the sky transmitting wonderful and terrible energies through our psyche. We must not remain asleep to them any longer. They are the secret messengers that we must come to know intimately because they reveal who we are and where we are going. They provide an opening into a time beyond this present moment and show us how wise or foolish we can be in making our next decision.

The knowledge of the planets that you are about to gain will help you in many different ways. **(See page 221 on how to order a computer printout of your planetary energies today. You will have it back in the mail in a few days and be able to use it with this book.)**

Benefits others have enjoyed

By understanding her daughter's planetary energies, a mother was relieved of her guilt and blame. Her young daughter was so demanding and manipulating that she thought it was her fault that she could not make her happy. I showed her how her daughter was born with the traits of anger, impatience, and willfulness. I explained that these conflicting energies were already in her daughter at birth and not a result of something she had done to her. Upon hearing this, a wall of tension left her face. She smiled. "Oh, I'm so relieved. I thought it was my fault. Now I understand a lot of things I didn't before. This really makes a lot of sense, because I couldn't find any reason for her to act that way. I was always puzzled by her behavior because I couldn't see how I caused it. This really changes my way of looking at her."

A man came to me once who was on the verge of suicide. I showed him how he was born naturally with a lot of self-doubt and the planetary energies that indicated this were under severe stress from other visiting planets at the time. I showed him when that energy would go away and that he would feel entirely different in a few weeks. I encouraged him to "hang in there" until this period of stress was over. He called me about a month later and thanked me for saving his life. I told him he saved his own life, but I was happy that I was there to help. "Well you did keep me from going mad," he insisted, "that saved my life."

The motion of the planets can also reveal an event that will occur in future time. If we calculate the motion and patterns of the planets at the time we ask a particular question, we can find the answer. I know this may sound absolutely ridiculous but how do you explain the following events?

In 1987, a married couple from California asked me if they should buy a particular piece of property. It sounded very idyllic with beautiful trees, flowers, and a running stream. I looked forward to giving them a strong "yes" answer, but after a thorough analysis of the planetary patterns forming at the time they asked the question, I could not tell them to buy the property. The planetary chemistry showed that the seller was devious and appeared to be hiding something from them. I also told them that the property was unstable. Something was wrong with it. Still, they were very upset with my answer because they really wanted to buy the property. I went back over the planetary positions for a promising sign because I felt badly for them. But the answer was still the same. I told them to consult a psychic or a geologist for another viewpoint because I could not change my mind. Several months later they called to tell me I was right after all. They had consulted a geologist and he told them that there had been a landslide on the property and that it was very young and unstable. They were grateful that I had pointed them to the right decision. They did not buy the property. In 1990, two years after they had moved to Arizona, they called and told me that the property I urged them not to buy was destroyed in 1989 by the Loma Prieta earthquake. It was one-quarter of a mile from the epicenter!

Once a business client asked me if he should sell his small business to a larger company, receive a cash equity of $250,000, and join the company as an executive. After analyzing the planetary chemistry that was forming at the time he asked the question, I said "No." "Are you sure?" he asked. "I could lose a lot of money if you're wrong." Since this was a very serious question with a lot of money at stake, I checked and double-checked my interpretation carefully. But the answer was the same. I said, "It will not work out. I don't see you doing it. You are not going to do it." But how could he turn down $250,000? He did. He soon found out that the potential buyers were very dishonest and "flaky" in their business dealings and he did not want to be associated with them. Here, again, the planets remained accurate in their message.

Once a lonely and desperate woman came to me and asked when she would meet her real lover. I searched through her birth patterns and found some very promising formations and concluded that a contact would take place in six months. I said, "On March 11, 1984, you will meet him. He will be very sensitive and artistic." Six months later, she quit her job and went to work in a hotel. On March 11, she met the hotel pianist and fell in love with him. The last time we talked, she said, "He's the one love of my life."

I must confess that I am not always this accurate. I do miss occasionally.

A man from Arizona was having trouble finding a woman to love. I said he would meet someone on St. Valentine's Day in 1987. The following year, sometime after the Valentine date, he called me and said he was upset with me. I asked, "Why?" He replied, "You said I would meet a girl on February 14 and I didn't. It was February the 12th!" We had a good laugh about me being two days off in my prediction.

There are literally hundreds of other stories, but this will give you an idea of the marvelous benefits we can gain from studying and living consciously with the planets. Although this book is not about prediction, you are about to learn how to see into the lives of other people, understand their hearts, motives, beliefs, and attitudes. You will quickly learn what your relationship is to your lover, friend, child, boss, or partner. When your own heart has been opened by the love process, your insights into these planetary energies will be greatly increased. You will gain a new depth of understanding because your own wisdom will be magnified. If you complete the journey laid out here, you will have the very best of two worlds: **The new wisdom and intelligence that comes from an open heart and a working knowledge of how to really understand other people.** This puts you in the best possible place to find the one you have always wanted.

5

The 12 Energy Fields of the Sun

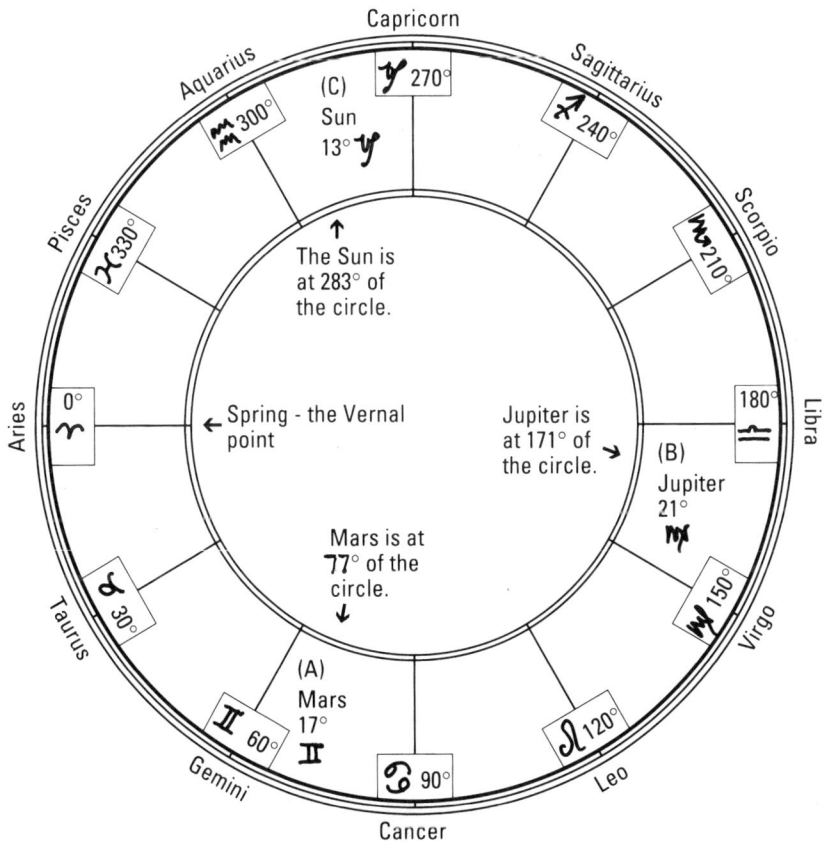

Figure I
This wheel shows the path of all the planets. Each 30 degree section of the path is a *solar energy field*.

In **Figure 1**, we see the path of the Sun, which is also the path of all the planets. This path is divided into 12 energy fields of 30 degrees apiece. I call these 30 degree arcs of space **solar energy fields** because they express the 12 unique human attitudes that are generated by the Sun's energy as it makes its yearly journey across the sky. Each solar energy field (30 degrees) has its own color or mood which is expressed in human consciousness as a way of looking at life. It is expressed as an **attitude**. It is important to understand that this is not the path of the stars or constellations which the ancient astronomers called "signs" (Aries, Taurus, Gemini, Cancer, Leo, Virgo, Libra, Scorpio, Sagittarius, Capricorn, Aquarius and Pisces), even though the solar fields have the same names. We are referring to the path of the Sun and its 12 circular energy fields and not the circular energy fields of the stars or constellations. We are not exploring the stars here, but the effect of the planets as they travel through the Sun's 12 energy fields. The first solar field begins when the Sun crosses the celestial equator and creates the Vernal or Spring Point. Even though this point moves slightly backward each year, it makes no difference for our purposes. It is still the starting point of the Sun's first energy field, Aries. (See a complete description of these solar energy fields starting on page 50.)

Planets pass through the solar energy fields according to their speed in orbit around the Sun (or from our perspective, around the Earth). The Moon travels around this entire circle within approximately 28 days but Pluto takes about 240 years to complete the journey. At the time you were born, various planets were scattered along this solar circle in probably several different energy fields. A planet at the time of your birth, could be anywhere along this circle. Let's look at a few examples:

Let us suppose that your date of birth shows that your Mars is at 17 degrees of Gemini. To find Mars' location on the 360 degree wheel, we start at the 60 degree point of

THE 12 ENERGY FIELDS OF THE SUN

the circle which is the same as 0 degree Gemini. You start counting at 0 degrees of Gemini (which is located at the 60 degree point of the sky's circle) and add 17 degrees. This gives you 77 degrees as the exact location of Mars along this circle. **(See A in Figure I on page 47.)** It is important to remember that each energy field starts at 0 degrees and ends at 30 degrees but it will start at a specific point on the 360 degree circle.

For another example, let's look at the energy field of Virgo which starts at 150 degrees of the circle. But this is also the starting degree of the Virgo energy field (0 degrees to 30 degrees). Your Jupiter is at 21 degrees of Virgo. What degree is Jupiter along the 360 degree circle? Simply add 21 to 150 which is 171. **(See B in Figure I.)** Let us try one more time.

Let us say that the Sun is at 13 degrees of the Capricorn energy field. At what degree is it located along the circle? We know that the Sun is found at 13 degrees of Capricorn, but what is its position along the 360 degree circle? First, you count from the start of Capricorn, which is 270 degrees and then you add 13 degrees, which gives you 283 degrees. **(See C in Figure I.)** It is important to keep these two perspectives clearly in mind.

Now that you understand how to locate a planet along this circle, you will need to determine the kind of effect or meaning the planets create in relationship to each other. (You may wish to copy the following descriptions of the 12 solar energy fields because you will be using them a lot in future chapters.)

The 12 energy fields of the Sun reveal our 12 basic human attitudes.

Field No: One
Name: Aries
Period: March 21 - April 19
Element: Fire
Color: Fire-Engine Red
Attitude: *Aggressive*
This fiery field imparts the attitude of aggression and enthusiasm in search of recognition. This is an aggressive "me first" attitude that rarely looks back. It concerns itself only with now and tomorrow and is quite open in its basic arrogance. There seems to be a lack of good judgment in the mere search of new challenges. It is the most powerful when energized by Mars or Pluto. Its positive influence is to initiate action and motivate others to new adventures. Its negative side is lack of discrimination, social ineptness, and failure to complete projects.

Field No: Two
Name: Taurus
Period: April 19 - May 20
Element: Earth
Color: Green
Attitude: *Possessive*
This earthy field imparts the attitude of possession and materialism. Its motive is to own things, acquire value (money and wealth), produce positive results, and to hold on to what it has acquired. There is a strong tendency toward sensual enjoyment that manifests itself in search of the finest foods, artistic pleasures, and sexual excesses. It has its most powerful effect when en-

THE 12 ENERGY FIELDS OF THE SUN

ergized by Venus (the desire to receive) and Jupiter (the desire to expand). Its positive side imparts a sense of loyalty and tenacity of purpose. The negative side tends toward lethargy, greed, and resistance to change.

Field No: Three
Name: Gemini
Period: May 21 - June 21
Element: Air
Color: Yellow
Attitude: *Communicative*

This airy field imparts the tendency to seek out clever, unique, and effective methods to communicate with others. This section of the solar field lends a fast mental facility and cleverness of ideas. There is a movement toward writing, speaking, teaching, journalism, or the arts. It has its most creative effect when energized by Mercury, the planet of speed, and rules the realm of logical processes. The positive side is ingenuity, cleverness, and alertness. Its negative side is inattention, restlessness, inconstancy, hypocrisy and "telling of tales."

Field No: Four
Name: Cancer
Period: June 22 - July 22
Element: Water
Color: Brown
Attitude: *Nurturing*

This water field of personal feelings gives the attitude of emotional security. Planets here energize the need for home, family, safety and preservation of tradition. There is a tendency to store up food, money and goods for the future

51

and a strong sentimental attachment to personal possessions. This field is greatly enlivened by the Moon, the planet which imparts the desire to sustain and nurture personal feelings. The positive qualities are caring for the family, thrift, and sensitivity to the protection of the home environment. Its negative expression is the selfish attitude of "me and mine," a crabby disposition, and seeking to fulfill personal needs without regard for others outside the family boundaries. There may be a smothering tendency.

Field No: Five
Name: Leo
Period: July 23 - August 22
Element: Fire
Color: Gold
Attitude: *Creative*

This fiery field is full of enthusiasm and imparts creative self-expression. A creative release of feeling is sought through the arts, children, entertainment, sports, romance, or risk-taking. There is a strong desire to seek the limelight and stay at the center stage of life. Some planets here give the urge to create a child, a work of art, or to pursue romance. The Sun is at home here. The positive expressions are artistic creations, a radiant countenance, and intense love for children. The negative side tends toward self-glorification, pride, and romantic self-indulgence without commitment of heart.

Field No: Six
Name: Virgo
Period: August 23 - September 22
Element: Earth
Color: Orange
Attitude: *Discriminative*

This earthy field relates strongly to practical matters. The dominant attitude here is practical management of detail in the form of service to a strong sense of discrimination and perfection. This solar field imparts a keen sense of discrimination which makes the individual strongly aware of human faults. The attention is focused on finding the most efficient way to function. But this tendency usually leads to strain which affects the mind and body because it is difficult to satisfy the compulsion for order, neatness, and correct behavior. The positive aspects are efficiency, cleanliness, and a willingness to be of service in helping others. The negative side tends toward overt criticism of self and others, an obsession with detail devoid of emotional connection to self and others, hypochondria, and straining the body and mind through overwork.

Field No: Seven
Name: Libra
Period: September 23 - October 23
Element: Air
Color: White
Attitude: *Relational*

This field has the quality of air which relates to social interactions and imparts the attitude of relationship. Relationship to one's spouse, partner, lover, and people everywhere. There is a strong tendency to belong to the group and share in its common goals. The attitudes of belonging, sharing, and relating with others are the primary expressions. There is often a tendency to find a balance in all relationships. If Venus is here, there may be a desire to create art forms that are perfectly balanced. The positive expressions are openness in relationship, fairness of action, good arbitration, and artistic awareness of beautiful forms and structures. The negative qualities are vanity, indecision, playing both ends against the middle, and reliance on others for happiness while using them selfishly to fulfill personal desires.

Field No: Eight
Name: Scorpio
Period: October 23 - November 22
Element: Water
Color: Black
Attitude: *Transforming*

This field has the quality of water which relates to emotional power and imparts the attitude of reserved intensity. Mars or Pluto here can raise this intensity to its highest expression where there is a tendency to struggle against self-limitation. The motives for self-transcendence are often in conflict with intense sexual/emotional impulses which highlight a struggle between light and darkness, or a sense of good and evil. (You will often find Scorpios wearing black and white together.) The positive qualities are intensity of purpose, self-transcendence, indomitable will, and loyalty to the underdog. The negative side shows a tendency toward sexual excesses, jealousy, sensitivity to criticism, deception, overt secrecy, and caution.

Field No: Nine
Name: Sagittarius
Period: November 23 - December 21
Element: Fire
Color: Blue
Attitude: *Expansive*

This field has the quality of fire which relates to an enthusiasm for adventure and exploration. This portion of the solar circle provides a strong social perspective. There is a need to reach out to the world, travel to foreign countries, probe philosophies, writing, religion, science, law, or higher education in pursuit of a broader perspective or understanding. There is a focus on principles, rather than on details or methods, and a restless need to go somewhere. The planet Jupiter here is strongest because it imparts the desire for expansion and exploration. The positive side lends a tendency toward truth, generosity, honesty, courage, and a straightforward expression of ideas. The negative side inclines toward harshness of speech, indifference to other people's feelings, bigotry, and a dangerous daredevil attitude.

Field No: Ten
Name: Capricorn
Period: December 22 - January 20
Element: Earth
Color: Gray
Attitude: *Managerial*

This field has the quality of the earth which relates to practical functions. It imparts a utilitarian tendency which seeks to make things useful. Therefore waste is not tolerated. The principles of management, power, and position tend to be primary expressions. It is a field of ambition, status, social position, and business. Saturn is very much at home here because it shows the desire to limit and define structure. The positive aspects are a sense of responsibility, duty, perseverance, and the ability to manage. The negative side is inclined toward stinginess, cruelty, indifference to the personal needs of others, and lack of enthusiasm for creative change.

Field No: Eleven
Name: Aquarius
Period: January 21 - February 19
Element: Air
Color: Blue-Green
Attitude: *Independence*

This field has the quality of air which relates to uniqueness of self-expression. This portion of the solar circle imparts the tendency toward change, innovation, and personal freedom in art, science, or social reform. There is a tendency to move to the edge of experience or be on the frontier of any project which a planet here may energize. Restrictions will not be tolerated and there is a need to break boundaries with tradition. Uranus is at home here because it lends the desire to innovation. The positive aspects are originality, helpfulness toward friends, and uniqueness of approach to new enterprises. The negative side is inclined toward mental arrogance, cruelty, emotional indifference, and inability to bond in a relationship.

THE 12 ENERGY FIELDS OF THE SUN

Field No: Twelve
Name: Pisces
Period: February 20 - March 20
Element: Water
Color: Purple
Attitude: *Ecstatic*

This field has the quality of water which relates to our most profound feelings. It imparts the tendency toward escape. There is an inclination toward seeking ecstasy and other-worldliness. The tendency is to move beyond where we are; to move toward something sublime or ecstatic. The material world tends to be ignored or denied. The emotional and visionary realm of the psyche seems to dominate. Neptune is strongest here because it reflects the desire for ecstasy. The positive attitudes are caring for others, self-forgetfulness, artistic imagination, and spiritual impulses. The negative side is shown in the fear of truth and responsibility, use of drugs for euphoric experiences, a weak will, deceit, and self-delusion.

The planets are always moving through these circular energy fields and energizing the attitudes of these fields. This means that if the Sun is in Cancer at the time of birth, a woman expresses an entirely different attitude toward a man than if her Sun was in Aquarius. The same holds true for all the other planets that travel through these fields. The planets manifest our attitudes.

6

The Impact of Planetary Energies

In Part I, you explored how to truly engage relationships. Now you will learn the chemistry of relationships and see how every person's attitudes are formed by the planets. You will discover your unique planetary patterns, your special qualities as a woman, and understand what kind of combinations create harmony or discord in all your relationships. We will be focusing on the five personal planets, the five transpersonal planets, and how they affect us. Let us now take a long look into our planetary world.

One of the personal planets is Mercury which is androgynous. Neutral. (We will consider Mercury later.) The other four consists of two masculine and two feminine energies. The Sun and Mars are masculine. The Moon and Venus are feminine. What we see when we look at a woman is the feminine (many types). What we see when we look at a man is the masculine (many types). But what is not generally seen is the man in the woman and the woman in the man.

The position of the Sun at the time of a woman's birth shows her heart — her inner man. The position of the Moon at the time of a man's birth, shows his heart — his inner woman. The position of a woman's Mars shows the kind of man she is attracted to sexually — her lover. The position of Venus in a man's chart shows the kind of woman he is attracted to sexually — his lover. When our heart and our passion are free of conflict and joined in harmony, then we are ready to engage our true lover — the one who belongs with us. The specific solar energy fields that the five personal planets were passing through at the time of your birth (Aries, Taurus, Gemini, etc.) and the kind of patterns they form with the five transpersonal planets show how you respond to love, intimacy and relationship.

The five transpersonal planets, Jupiter, Saturn, Uranus, Neptune, and Pluto have a tremendous effect on the Sun, Moon, Venus, Mars, and Mercury when they come in contact with them. But what is meant by contact?

Since all the planets travel along the same 360 degree circle in the sky and are moving at different velocities, they make contact with each other in several ways.

1. **The five transpersonal planets stimulate the personal planets in a positive or negative way according to where they are found at birth.** This is what you were born with. These planetary combinations are locked into your psyche. They are you. This is the way you are. You will soon understand how this works.

2. **The transpersonal planets of one person stimulates the personal planets of another.** The planetary combinations between you and another person tell you whether you can relate harmoniously with them or not. Here each of your planetary systems are affecting each other. Your relationship can arouse many feelings that you may have never felt before. The impact of the other person's planets creates a different chemistry within you when they are combined with yours. These energies either enhance and support your relationship or obstruct it. This is what is called "taking on the karma of another person." This karma may be positive or negative.

3. **The personal planets are stimulated by the transpersonal planets presently moving in the sky.** I call these visiting planets. Although some visiting planets

THE IMPACT OF PLANETARY ENERGIES

bring temporary passing events, others can have an effect that lasts for several years but eventually comes to an end. Such experiences can range from a few happy hours with our lover to many years of obstruction, transformation, or support in abundance and opportunity.

These three primary contacts reveal the positive and negative experiences of our life. (For the sake of simplicity, we will not be exploring the effect that the transpersonal planets have on each other.)

When people have a positive or negative relationship, they may never suspect that planetary energies are behind their harmony or frustration. I often see people going through very frustrating periods who have no idea what forces within them are being activated. They simply call it life and curse the day. Sometimes, I have tried to explain what is really happening, but they usually give me a strange look and walk away.

The planetary patterns between people tell us what we really need to know about their relationship. This means that we can explain the nature of their relationship before they even meet! Think of the potential for business, marriage or any kind of partnership. When managers put people together they would know how to match them up to get the best results. Potential partners could save miles of paper consumed in lawsuits by avoiding those people who would be their adversary. (Of course, this means that some lawyers would have to find a different line of work.) It is really no mystery why people like or dislike each other when we view their relationship from a study of their combined planetary patterns. These combined planetary patterns show the true relationship quite clearly.

Every once in a while I hear a story in the news that a Hindu family consulted a celestial matchmaker to pick a husband for their daughter. This procedure tends to shock us in the West because most of us prefer to use our own instincts to find our mate. In the last story I heard, I was told that the couple fell in love instantly upon meeting each other for the first time. While I have never tracked these arrangements, there may be some lesson we can learn in the West about how we go about choosing our mates since nearly 65% of married Americans get divorced.

When we discover the planetary pictures of people at the time of their birth, we are using patterns that are more or less fixed as their basic nature. Some patterns can be changed by heart-opening experiences. Such people show remarkable transformations in their attitudes. But without such experiences, most people don't seem to change that much. It appears for the most part that real change is the result of something that happens to us; not something we deliberately bring about. For example, most of us would not deliberately choose to become totally vulnerable emotionally to another person, but if our love for them was so overwhelming that we had nothing to say in the matter, and could not prevent ourselves from making that gesture of love, we could be completely transformed by the experience. No matter how painful it might be. There is no doubt that we would see love entirely differently as a result of such an experience and would probably be deeply transformed by it. This is certainly the way to the wonderful secret I describe earlier in this book. A mystery that is solved once we understand our masculine or feminine heart.

7

The Four Planetary Effects

The impact of planetary energies is made in many different ways, but the most important effects are the conjunction, sextile, square, and trine. (Of course, there is the opposition, quincunx and a whole batch of other effects but they are too complex for the purpose of this book. We need to stay as simple as possible without sacrificing the benefits.) These four major effects are best explained by looking at the 360 degree circle. (See Figure 1, page 47.)

1. **The Conjunction** - The effect of the conjunction (0 degrees) is INTENSIFICATION. The planets involved unite to form an intensified energy. While this energy may be subtle or obvious, it is still intensified. An analysis of the planets involved tell us how the energy is manifested; whether it is positive or negative. A conjunction occurs when two or more planets are found within 10 degrees plus or minus of each other and found in the same energy field. (This variation from exact is called "orb" of influence and is not a precise rule. You will have to experiment with what seems to be true from your own experience. Others may disagree.) This means that if Venus is found at 23 degrees of Leo and Saturn is 29 degrees of Leo, the planets are in conjunction. If Saturn is also at 23 degrees of Leo, then this conjunction is exact. If Saturn is at 0 degrees of Virgo,

it is still only 7 degrees away from Venus, but because it is in a different energy field, it is not a conjunction. (Virgo is the next energy field that follows Leo.) To form a conjunction, planets must be in the same energy field. Even if the planets are only 1 to 10 degrees apart yet are in different energy fields, they are not conjunct. For example, if a planet is at 1 degree of Cancer and another planet is at 29 degrees of Gemini, the previous energy field, they are not conjunct, even though they are only 2 degrees apart. Here are examples of planets **not** in conjunction:

- Mars at 29 degrees Pisces and Uranus at 1 degree of Aries (the next energy field)
- The Sun at 5 degrees of Gemini and Neptune at 28 degrees of Taurus (the previous energy field)

Note: If the two planets are in different energy fields they are not in conjunction no matter how close they are. They are manifesting different attitudes and therefore they cannot be intensified or joined together. This would be like trying to blend oil and water.

2. **The Sextile** - The effect of the sextile (60 degrees) in a relationship is CREATIVE. It is also harmonious like the trine but seems to offer more stimulation for creative activity. The energies between the two planets are very positive and supportive. A sextile occurs when two planets are within 60 degrees of each other plus or minus 10 degrees on each side. However, it the 10 degree orb puts one of these planets in the third energy field away, they are not sextile. If Mars is at 24 degrees of Aries and the Uranus is at 1 degree of Cancer, they are not sextile. If Uranus was at 24 degrees of Gemini, it would be exactly sextile with Mars. Even though 1 degree of Cancer is only 67 degrees from 24 degrees of Aries, Uranus has moved into the third field away from Aries and manifest more of a hostile energy

THE FOUR MAJOR PLANETARY EFFECTS

in the Cancer water field because Aries is fire. Fire and water do not go together. These planets are not sextile. If the Sun is at 3 degrees of Libra and Uranus is at 8 degrees Sagittarius, they are sextile. If the Moon is at 19 Scorpio and Saturn is at 14 degrees of Virgo, they are sextile. (If you have forgotten how to calculate this, please review Chapter 5.) It is important to note that no matter what distance these planets are from each other **within these energy fields** they still function harmoniously with each other. The reason for this is because they are found in energy fields that are harmonious. Libra is air and Sagittarius is fire. Fire and air go well together. Virgo is earth and Scorpio is water. These elements work well with each other. Therefore, it is important to remember that even though they may not be sextile according to our rule, they still work harmoniously together. However, for the sake of simplicity and to avoid confusion, stick to the 10 degree orb rule.

    3.   **The Square** - The effect of the square (90 degrees) is FRUSTRATION. I consider it the most difficult energy to work with, and those people born with planetary "squares" certainly know the meaning of frustration. The difficulty is that the planets are expressing attitudes that are not in harmony with each other. The needs are in conflict. Planets are in square relationship if they are 90 degrees apart, plus or minus 1 to 10 degrees on either side. (Unless, of course, they cross over into the next energy field as described under the sextile interpretation.) If Mars is in Capricorn at 9 degrees and Pluto is in Libra at 9 degrees, they are exactly square. Likewise, if Mars is at 4 degrees and Pluto is at 9 degrees, they are also square. Notice that the energy fields of Capricorn and Libra are earth and air. These are not compatible elements in nature. Air stirs up the earth. When it turns to a wind or a tornado, it can violently affect the earth. If planets are not within the "orb" of a square, they are still considered to be frustrating en-

ergies unless the orb takes them into another field as previously described.

4. **The Trine** - The effect of the trine (120 degrees) is FULFILLMENT. It is considered the best relationship possible between planets. But, strange as it may sound, you don't want too many trines between your planets. Life becomes too easy and there is little stimulus to grow. Trines do not build character but they sometimes bring blessings. A trine occurs when two planets are within 120 degrees, plus or minus 10 degrees on either side. (Except you must remember the rule of crossing over into another field when an orb is used.) Venus at 1 degree Taurus is trine Neptune at 1 degree of Capricorn. Venus at 21 degrees of Gemini is trine Saturn at 16 degrees Aquarius. Venus at 12 degrees of Cancer is trine Pluto at 17 degrees of Scorpio. Planets in the same element but in different energy fields are very harmonious with each other. (There are three earth, three fire, three water, and three air fields.) If you have Venus in Leo (fire) at 20 degrees and Jupiter in Sagittarius (fire) at 20 degrees, the planets are not only trine but both are also in fire energy fields. (Review Chapter 4.) Planets found in the same element are always trine or conjunct.

8

The Five Personal Planets in the Twelve Energy Fields

The information that follows describes the five personal planets in their most pure and simple form. However, we need to keep in mind that they are more complex in meaning when combined and related to another planet. Together, they become something different than when functioning alone. When a woman combines the meaning (or voice) of another planet related to her Sun, for example, she will gain a deeper understanding of how she is constructed emotionally toward men, how free she is in relationship, or what her basic obstructions are to real love and intimacy. This is because the heart of a woman is shown by the Sun. So, keep in mind that the blend is different from a single planetary voice. Planets express themselves internally as the silent dialogues we have with ourselves. Therefore, they are experienced as voices from within. (More about this in Chapter 14.) Two planets together create a unique dialogue for us to understand. We will explore how the five personal planets (Sun, Moon, Venus, Mars, and Mercury) express the attitudes of the twelve energy fields of the Sun. Then we will combine them with the transpersonal planets (Jupiter, Saturn, Uranus, Neptune, and Pluto). You will learn how these combinations deter-

THE HEART OF A MAN IS A WOMAN

mine the nature of your internal dialogues — your planetary voices. (**If you have not done so, remember to order the computer printout of your planetary patterns now. See page 221.**) You will need your personal printout of your planets to learn how to combine your patterns for interpretation.

Example Interpretation

For an example in interpretation, we will use the chart of a woman born in 1945 (specific birth data omitted). Here is a computer printout of her planetary patterns that was produced by the *Skyclock* program.

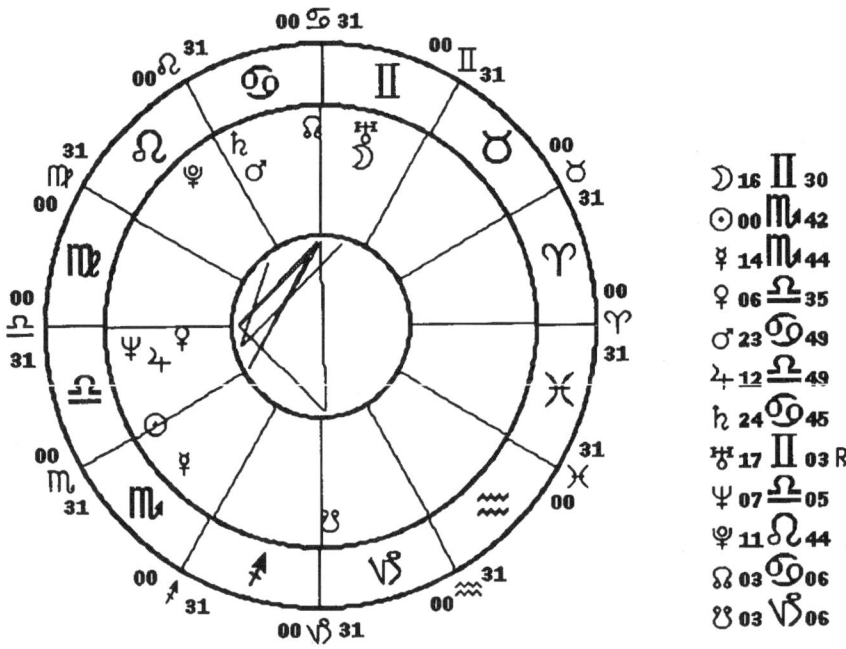

THE FIVE PERSONAL PLANETS IN THE 12 ENERGY FIELDS

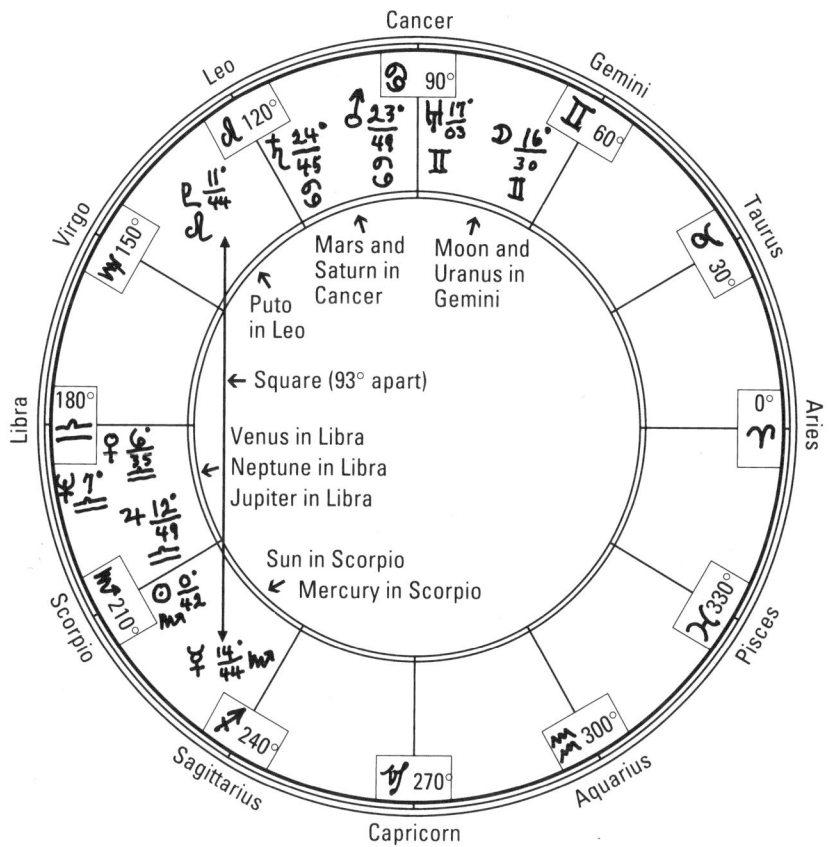

For the sake of simplicity, we have extracted the positions of her planets from the printout and put them in the wheel above to show their primary relationships. If you have not already done so, please copy the **12 Energy Fields** from Chapter 5 to have handy for your analysis. You will be using this information in conjunction with the material in this chapter.

The most prominent features in this chart are four conjunctions and one square. The Moon in Gemini is conjunct Uranus in Gemini, Mars is conjunct Saturn in Cancer, Venus is conjunct Jupiter in Libra and Neptune in Libra, and Mercury in Scorpio is square Pluto in Leo.

Venus as a voice by herself in the Libra solar field, loves people and relationships. See **Venus in Libra** on page 103. But notice that Venus is next to Jupiter which adds a very positive feeling to Libra (note they are about 6 degrees apart). Since the conjunction here is not a conflict, this is a very supportive energy for having good friends, and feeling sustained by the world. See **Jupiter's positive effects on Venus** on page 140. Her inner dialogue might be something like "I feel supported by my friends and feel they will always be there for me. If one love does not work out, I know I will find another one." This is an unusual pattern because we have another planet that joins the two — Neptune. Since Neptune is a very high and subtle energy, its connection here tends to exalt Venus. "I desire to have a spiritual relationship with another. I long for my soul mate. I am very idealistic in love. I love all things beautiful and artistic."

See **Neptune's positive effects on Venus,** pages 158-159.

Our next pattern shows the Moon to be conjunct Uranus. This is an unusual combination because these two planets are very different in character. The Moon seeks security and comfort while Uranus seeks the unknown and loves to live on the edge. When we put these two energies together, we get "I feel good when I am always moving toward the next experience. I cannot stand old ideas, habits and daily routines that repeat themselves. I get my security from moving on." See page 151 for **Uranus' positive effects on the Moon**. Here the larger planet, Uranus dominates the mental attitude of the Moon in Gemini. This is a very restless energy.

Now, you do the next two patterns: Mars conjunct Saturn and Mercury square Pluto. Since a conjunction between Mars and Saturn is basically negative, see pages

147-148 for a description of this combination. Note how this combination affects this woman's feelings toward men. If you run across a woman who has this pattern, you will be able to confirm the difficulty she has with men.

The Mercury square Pluto is also a difficult planetary pattern. Do you remember how the square is determined (90 degrees)? Since Mercury is the faster moving planet, we relate its position to the slower moving Pluto. Mercury had just passed its exact square to Pluto and is now 93 degrees away from Pluto. But this is still a square. See **Pluto's negative effect on Mercury** on page 170. What do you think this woman would be saying to herself? What is her basic mental attitude? I will give you one phrase: **Mental intolerance**. Again, you can confirm your analysis by looking for people who have this planetary pattern and seeing what they are like. In fact, when you begin to discover that people respond exactly the way the planets say they will, you will be very pleased. Where else could you find such an accurate system for understanding human nature?

THE SUN

The Sun is considered a planet because it represents a specific principle in our life and gives us the desire to survive. It is pure masculinity in nature. It rules the force behind all creative action because it gives life to the other planets. It represents authority and those in power. It is sheer energy, without complication, but it does not express itself so easily in people that way. It is strongly connected to the ego because it manifests as the desire to be alive, to survive, and to be recognized by others. It is colored by the particular solar field it is found in at birth, which is expressed in the form of personal attitudes, biases, and opinions — an internal voice. The Sun has dominion over children, (your creations), romance, speculation, spirit of adventure, men, and creativity.

The location of the Sun at the moment of birth reveals a woman's true heart nature — the man inside. The Sun is the heart of a woman. Therefore, the heart of a woman is a man. The man is the masculine form of the heart of a woman, but the core of her heart is actually beyond male and female. This core is the soul, which is represented by Pluto. (We will explore this later in Chapter 11.) The Sun is an initiating force. The father archetype. The life-giver. Whatever solar field the Sun was passing through at the time of your birth, indicates the kind of man who holds the greatest attraction for you and who would most likely reflect your heart. (Think of a solar field as an attitude — a specific kind of internal voice. It shows the way a planet expresses itself. What attitude that planet has in expressing its desires.) This is why the Sun is so important in helping you understand what you like in a man, the man who is best for you, and what his attitudes should be. The Sun of your birthchart reveals your inner man. The outer man you are attracted to should be in harmony with your inner man. But this is seldom true in most relationships.

The Sun is a direct link to the kind of man a woman will love because he will reflect her heart and enliven her being — make her feel alive. She is drawn to that which she is already. For example, if her Sun is in the solar field of Gemini at the time of her birth (born between May 21 and June 21) she is drawn to a bright and shiny man who is charming, witty, clever, intensely curious and always in search of new ideas. She likes a man who never stands still, because this is the nature of her own heart. The Sun for a woman is the voice of love. In its pure form without complication, it is not confused with desire or need. It is love simply, willing to shine forth, unable to ask for anything because it is fullness itself. Along with Pluto, the Sun is the woman's inmost feeling nature. It is the voice of her heart. However, her sun (heart) may be obstructed by another planet and make it difficult for her to relate intimately with the man she is really attracted to. When the Sun is blended with another planet the attitudes and feelings of the heart will be affected in that woman according to the nature of the planet which relates to it. (You will be learning all about this shortly.) You may wish to skip to Chapter 9 and refer to this section again when you get to the stage of analyzing planetary patterns.

SUN IN THE 12 SOLAR FIELDS

Sun In The Aries Solar Field - Fiery Red
A Fire Field
KEY PHRASE:
> "I am aggressive, arrogant, and adventurous. I like to try new things and want to be first."

If your Sun is in the Aries solar field, you were born in a very powerful energy field which is represented most strongly by fire-engine red. It imparts a very aggressive spirit and attitude. (Do you love red cars?) When the Sun is found here, you have a very aggressive approach to experiences. You would love a man with such a spirit because he would reflect your masculine nature. You would not be able to tolerate weak and passive men. However, you could attract such men, if you have a deep fear of being vulnerable to a man who is a "tiger." If you have the need to stay in control, and have a deep fear of letting your heart go, you will attract men you can dominate. In this case, you would be going against your own heart nature and choose to be the tiger yourself. In a sense, you would be at war with your own power. You would eventually have to embrace the "tiger" man and let him be who he is without being at war with him. This could be your road to happiness. If this is the case, you would have to stop avoiding strong men and choose to embrace them, or process your relationships with them until you become clear on what you want from a man and what he is really like inside of yourself. As an Amazonian woman you must eventually embrace the tiger-man and lay down your sword by understanding in your heart that you no longer need to be at war with him. You will be glad to give up the struggle and happy to let him be who he is: A FIERY GO-GETTER.

Sun In The Taurus Solar Field - Green An Earth Field

KEY PHRASE:
> *"I am tenacious, sensual, and earthy. I need to take my time and cannot be pushed."*

When your Sun is in this field, its fiery impulse is slowed down because this is a very earthy energy. Your primary attitude points towards the good things of the earth. You have strong desires for money, food, sensuality, acquisition, and loyalty in relationship. Therefore, you are looking for this kind of man. He will be dear to your heart, if he fulfills your worldly requirements. When you find him, he will reflect your heart. He will fill the inside of you with great comfort and he will feel as close to you as your breath. You will love him because he is loyal, true-blue, tenacious, sensual, and a good provider. Tradition and the need for predictability are strong in your own nature and you will be attracted to the man who reflects these desires. You have strong aversions to change, because once your feelings are set on something, it is difficult to get you to feel any other way. There is a strong stubbornness and resistance to change.

A man with his Sun in Taurus may seldom say that he loves you, but he will show you in many ways, and assumes that you know he does. You may also be the same way. He can tend to be a "couch potato" and somewhat lethargic at times (slow to move) but you probably won't mind this because you would have great tolerance toward him and often may not feel like doing anything yourself. However, there could be some problems in your relationship if you have your Mars in the fiery energy field of Leo or the airy field of Aquarius because these energies are in conflict with the Taurus energy. The Leo side of your nature would demand that your lover "get off his can and do something," or your Aquarian Mars would reflect your own internal conflicts with the possessive attitude of Taurus and the detached attitudes of Aquarius. These combinations make for complexity and confusion in relationships and need to be understood. Soon you will learn how to combine these conflicting planetary energies and see how they work in relationship. It is a fascinating discovery.

Sun In The Gemini Solar Field - Yellow
An Air Field

KEY PHRASE:
> "I am clever, quick-witted, and restless. I need to communicate and do many things at once. I have a hard time finishing things."

With your Sun in the Gemini solar field, your heart tends to be in your head. You are attracted to bright and clever men who are witty, exciting, and unpredictable but may not be very grounded in practical matters nor committed to you in any meaningful way. You may have trouble being really intimate yourself because of an inherent fear of being bound or held accountable in a relationship. You tend to be involved with more than one man at a time because you not only like to keep your options open but are not quite sure where your feelings lie. To commit yourself to one relationship is to deny the possibility of the other, so you tend to put off making a decision as long as you can. But sooner or later, you will be confronted with making a choice and have to do some real soul-searching. What is actually going on is that you really prefer to have two men to avoid being stuck with only one. The whole idea of one is a lifelong challenge for you, because deep in your heart you prefer two choices in just about everything. You will tend to attract fickle men because they reflect your own conflict with intimacy. Fortunately, you are not just one planet, so there are other options. You can have an intense love for and heart connection to a Gemini man if he has his own Mars or Venus conjunct your Pluto (in the same solar field). If your Pluto is at 25 degrees of Leo, and his Venus or Mars is in the same place, there can be an intense physical and emotional connection between you in spite of the tendency for both of you to "live in your head." The reason being that Pluto in your chart is your very soul and any man whose Sun makes a contact with this planet will always be a special person to you and could end up being your "soul" mate. We will be taking a closer look at this planet later.

Sun In The Cancer Solar Field - Brown
A Water Field

KEY PHRASE:
> *"I am sensitive, nurturing, and crabby. I need a home and family. I have to feel safe and secure."*

If you were born when the Sun was traveling through the Cancer solar field, you have a lot of personal emotions and feelings. This is the field of the mother archetype. It is also a field of water which is the realm of personal emotions. Your heart is centered on the home, children, family, food, the stomach, patriotism, tradition, security, and perpetuating your own cultural background: your family. This solar field shows that you want a mate with the same attitudes because these are the things that are dearest to your heart. He will be emotional, sensitive, moody, and somewhat maternal in nature because Cancer tends towards mothering and nesting. He will probably have a strong connection to his mother, his own family, and value the same things that you do. However, if he is not mature emotionally, he may expect you to be his mother, and this could spell trouble. Since you have a very strong mothering instinct, you could fall into this trap. Of course some Cancers like being the big mother. This gives them power and control, but these attitudes have nothing to do with love and the heart. You will have to resist trying to mother your man even if he tries to put you in that mold. It is necessary that he find his own strength within himself. You have to resist the temptation to maintain control by keeping him a boy. This will be a test for you because your nurturing instinct is quite strong. You have to separate nurturing from (s)mothering. This does not mean you cannot offer support, but be aware that you don't want to play the mother-boy game with your mate nor try to manipulate him emotionally. Don't try to keep him the boy so you can be the mother and play the superior role as the great giver. Your challenge is to release him to himself and not try to direct his actions. Objectivity and truth in feelings and needs must forever be your practice in order to experience true intimacy and strength in your love relationship.

Sun In The Leo Solar Field - Gold
A Fire Field
KEY PHRASE:
> "I am proud, creative, and romantic. I like being at the center of attention and have to be in charge."

The Sun is very much at home here because Leo is also a fiery energy field. When I describe the man you are most attracted to, I am really talking about you. Remember, the heart of a woman is a man (masculine). The man you are attracted to reflects your own heart nature or your own internal conflicts toward men. That which you love and feel as an overwhelming attraction, is a male energy that is most in tune with your own heart nature. Your male self is strong, radiant, proud, dramatic, and in love with love itself. You want a strong, lionhearted guy to match your need to be at the center of the action and to express an open heart. You feel that you should hold a place of respect and find menial tasks or inferior positions intolerable. You are very proud and expect to be honored. You can be bossy and domineering because your male self is very strong. Since this is the Queen/King energy field, you tend to "lord" it over others. But if you are too much this way, then the Sun in your chart may be afflicted by other planets, showing deep conflicts in your own heart toward men and therefore you respond with contempt and competition. Actually, any of these tendencies to dominate or manipulate other men show that your relationship to your inner male is neither peaceful nor harmonious. You would be at war with him, and until these inner tensions are resolved, you would continue to attract those men whom you can control and dominate because you do not want to be vulnerable to their power. You would tend to avoid the kind of man who is sure of himself and at peace with his own inner woman. At the same time, you might feel a tremendous attraction to him but be terrified of the possibility of losing control or being vulnerable. The lesson here is to engage such a relationship because it has the most to teach you. Such a relationship can open you up on the deepest level and put you in touch with what real love is all about. Giving our heart to another is sometimes terrifying but it is important to remember that only by losing our heart do we find it.

Sun In The Virgo Solar Field - Orange
An Earth Field

KEY PHRASE:
> *"I am helpful, picky, and efficient. I love a job well done and am very hard on myself."*

If your Sun was in the solar field of Virgo at the time of your birth, you are born with a very practical nature. You really like a man who has it together: neat, proper, efficient, helpful, dutiful, and organized. You are very hard on yourself because of perfectionist tendencies. Nothing is ever really right. Everything needs to be corrected and done perfectly. This is what you expect from your mate. But you need to ask, "Where is the emotion? The feeling? The heart?" Are you reacting to being too emotional or self-serving out of fear of losing your togetherness? Your mind is usually very sharp and you honor the finest things in life, but the man you are looking for is more of a mental and practical person than a romantic. In fact, you often prefer a man who is not so romantic. It may just be too "mushy" for you. Do you feel that such open emotions are a fault? Are efficiency, order, and perfection more important than the heart? Certainly these functions have to do more with the mental realm than the heart realm. However, if a potential mate has his Venus, Mars or Neptune next to your Sun, he can arouse the opposite side of you (Pisces) and move you beyond your overt need for perfection and habits of self-criticism. Further, there can be other connections in the chart that can offset the dry, practical attitudes of merely trying to keep your life perfect and together. You need a little wildness. Sheer abandonment to your lover without thinking too much would be an exercise to your benefit. In short, you need to be moved beyond your need to control the mind and keep everything so squeaky clean.

Sun In The Libra Solar Field - White
An Air Field

KEY PHRASE:
> "I am social, artistic, and indecisive. I love being with people and want harmony and beauty in relationships."

The attitudes of this solar field have to do with relationships. You are drawn to the beautiful, the artistic, the just, the fair, and the ideal loving situation, because this is the way you are in your heart. There is some tendency to pretend that everything is okay even though the evidence is otherwise. You hate discord and conflict, so you are good at arbitrating. You like to look at opposing viewpoints and bring them into balance. It is difficult for you to stick to one side of an issue, because you feel the other side could be right. You can usually find a case for both. But this tendency can cause problems in relationship because you don't really seem to take a strong stand for anything. This wavering can lead others to break off with you. The group, belonging and sharing with others, is very important to you. Solitude is not something you can live with unless you are engrossed in the creative act of making music, designing, decorating, writing, or painting. Beauty and harmony are very necessary to your sense of well-being. If these elements are missing in your life, you can become very unhappy. A man who is good looking, pleasant, cooperative, just, social, artistic, charming, and sensitive will appeal to your heart nature. What is important to realize here is that the man I am describing is a reflection of yourself. If your own heart is clear on what you need and who you are, the man in your life will truly reflect that.

Sun In The Scorpio Solar Field - Black
A Water Field

KEY PHRASE:
> "I am intense, possessive, and critical. I love being my own boss and need to be in control of my feelings."

This solar field is permeated with a deep emotional water energy and is probably the most mysterious of all the fields. Scorpio is so deep in meaning that an ordinary awareness cannot comprehend the depth of the subtleties it imparts. Often, you will appear to others to be someone you are not. That's why you are misunderstood. However, you tend not to let others inside of your skin. You consider that this would be too much of an advantage for them to have. The truth is that your heart is profoundly sensitive, intense, loyal, and deep. But not everyone knows that. You have an inherent reluctance to being known and have tremendous resistance to change. You are attracted to a man who will reflect these depths but he will be just as reluctant as you when it comes to revealing himself. He has a mysterious charisma that pulls you into yourself. You will tend to attract men who are not emotionally vulnerable because they will have a reluctance to say how they feel. Many of them don't know how they feel because their feelings are suppressed. They will wait for you to make the first move. But you generally wait for them to make the first move. This is especially true if you have not discovered how to be vulnerable yourself. Your Scorpio heart is one of great reluctance. It does not want to submit itself totally to intimacy. Even though you may intensely desire such intimacy, your great pride works against it. This is the way of the

Scorpion. However, since 1984, the Scorpio nature has been going through many emotional transformations that have opened the heart and put the Scorpio woman in touch with her deepest pains. This is due to Pluto's journey through the Scorpio energy field for the last ten years. Pluto's transit in Scorpio will continue until the work is complete by 1996. You have the greatest capacity for expressing the deepest love of all the energy fields, but you need to embrace intimacy from the heart and not just the body. Your lifelong motto and practice should be: "I am willing to be known."

Sun In The Sagittarius Solar Field - Sky Blue A Fire Field

KEY PHRASE:
> "I am straightforward, blunt, and restless. I love to travel and look for new adventures just over the mountain."

Your heart is the heart of the adventurer. You love truth and honesty. You have an intense aversion to weakness. So the man who stirs your heart is also forthright, speaks his mind, works hard, plays hard, and has great energy for action. Like you, he loves to travel and explore distant countries and foreign cultures. You have an interest in learning, education, publishing, law, and philosophy. You have a restless spirit. You're not much for sitting, dreaming, and pondering. You are a "now" person who responds to immediate action and activity. You probably love to walk and find sports challenging, stimulating and entertaining. If you are intuitively advanced, you will look for understanding and probe the greater mysteries of life. You will search far and wide for the meaning of life and explore the spiritual realms through meditation and contemplation. You may be attracted to another type of man who likes the outdoors where he can hunt, fish, and test his courage to explore the unknown. Whatever kind of man you are attracted to, he will stand as an inner mirror to your heart nature. Because of your dominant spirit, you must avoid men who cannot challenge you. Yet, like the Aries woman, you may be attracted to weak men because they are easy to control and you don't have to be vulnerable. You may get a sense of power from doing this but, in the end, you will only suffer disappointment over these choices. To more fully understand how your heart needs are expressed on these levels, you will need to explore the relationship of your Sun to the other planets in your chart. By the time you finish this book, you should be thoroughly familiar with your needs.

Sun In The Capricorn Solar Field - Gray
An Earth Field

KEY PHRASE:
"I am serious, dedicated, and sensible. I love tradition and am ambitious to find my place in the world."

This is a solar field of the father archetype. Capricorn is an earthly solar field that is compatible with the Taurus and Virgo solar fields. It gives practical, pragmatic, and utilitarian tendencies such as, "If I can't use it, throw it away." This is the symbol of the goat, and you love to "go-at" things that are a challenge. You don't back down easily and are often quite firm in your convictions. The group is more important than the individual, and if an individual offends or is not responsible toward the group, company or association, you are willing to act ruthlessly to get rid of him. You identify with the older man of tradition, ambition, achievement, social status, and power. You honor integrity and responsibility and are very conscientious of the work at hand. This field tends to make you want to keep the status quo. You try to build on what went before but usually within the same mold. The man you love is stable, predictable, and ambitious. Since these are the attitudes within your own heart, this is the kind of male company you will tend to attract in your life. There may be a strong attachment to the father or memories of an austere childhood where you were expected to handle responsibilities that were beyond your maturity. If this is the case, you don't expect things to be given to you. You probably feel that you have to earn everything you do get. You are the one person who knows that you don't get something for nothing. Letting go of expectations for the sake of real love may be your greatest challenge. The Cancer solar field may be your best partner, because they will provide the warm, family hearth where you can place your heart. You need to practice the art of foolishness and be more wild at heart. For more information relating to your heart nature, explore the relationships that other planets form with your Sun. (See Chapter 9.)

Sun In The Aquarius Solar Field - Blue Green An Air Field

KEY PHRASE:

> *"I am opinionated, cool, and detached. I love my friends, but I love my freedom most of all."*

The man you will love is certainly unpredictable. He is a free spirit who follows his own drumbeat. He does not possess a very deep emotional energy. Love here is based mostly on friendship and the thrill of exploring new boundaries in sex and relationship. It is always the future that holds the greatest promise for you, so you try to make sure that your options remain open to take advantage of the new opportunities ahead. It is probably true to say that you are the one person who does not look back. If you do, then it is probably only briefly. The next experience, relationship or possibility is what holds your interest. You have no sentimentality or gushy feelings. Everything is rather cut and dried. It either is or it isn't. There is not much in between. You are extremely honest and sometimes brutally frank and cruel without meaning to be. But you often speak abruptly without discrimination and offend those who may be close to you. You cannot endure any demands or restrictions that others may try to press upon you. It is difficult to form lasting bonds with one person because of your need to remain free, detached, and uncommitted. You like your friends but you don't want to be bound by them. Romance and true intimacy may be two separate paths for you. But your challenge is to bring them together. The sign you have most to learn from in this regard is probably Leo, because they radiate the heart warmth that you need in order to feel connected emotionally. Your relationship to a man has to be unique and unusual because you do not fit into any conventional mold where you are expected to conform to other people's expectations. You can be very magnetic and attractive to others, but they often fool themselves when they think they can capture your heart. You would never be happy with a conventional man. He has to always be a challenge, exciting, interesting and keeping you guessing. In short, you love him because you can't have him. He always keeps you guessing. But God help him if he ever becomes predictable. You could be gone by nightfall.

Sun In The Pisces Solar Field - Purple
A Water Field

KEY PHRASE:
> *"I am sensual, sentimental, and sacrificial. I feel deeply about other people's pain and have a need to escape from the world."*

This is the solar field of the mystic, the psychic, the dreamer, the con man/woman, artist, filmmaker, alcoholic, nurse, or saint. Your heart resides in another world and you tend toward men who live in another world. But you may carry too much guilt and burdens from the past to be free enough to have a concrete understanding of what kind of man you want. You can become trapped by the man who needs your help because you are like Mother Teresa looking to save the destitute. Your description of the man you like can be quite indefinite and nebulous. You may say something like, "I want him to be emotional and sensitive." But how about responsible! You need to add that virtue to your list in looking for your mate. The difficulty is that you are so accepting of men and friends that you cannot distinguish the faults from the virtues. You are vulnerable because you are too open. You may have to carry men who are "flakes" on your shoulders for a long time before you realize that they are not what you thought they were and they are really using you. You really have a deep aversion to the cold reality of the world, so to protect yourself against it, you can pretend everything's sublime. You need to learn to embrace the truth, discard those dewy-eyed glasses, test your dreams, and crush them if they don't work. If you are clear in your heart who you are emotionally, then you can have the deepest loving relationship. But clarity means you have no illusions about the kind of man who is best for you. In order to get this clarity, you will need to engage men on a very realistic level. In other words, you may have to look at them two or three times and judge them against a solid standard of conduct. This will help you "process" your relationships to the point of clarity. You probably have the greatest capacity of all for loving and giving but your challenge will be to make it real; to actualize it in human terms.

THE MOON AND VENUS

It is important to understand the differences between the Moon and Venus, because their descriptions sound similar. The Moon is the great mother — the giver of the milk.

Venus is the goddess of the feminine. She rules all that is beautiful, delicate, refined, as well as love and relationships. The Moon is a man's heart and Venus is his feminine ideal. Both reveal the kind of woman he needs and desires. Without these very human planets, he would have no food or love.

A woman's feminine self is shown by Venus and the Moon. While the Moon relates to the mother, Venus relates to feelings of self-worth. The Moon and Venus work closely together because they show our feelings and work to sustain us on earth. They are feminine energies because they embody nurturing, sustaining, preserving, caring, and relating. These two planets are more externalized in a woman and internalized in a man. However, they show the emotional relationship to the mother in both sexes. These two planets hold the key to a man's feminine self. The Moon is his heart and Venus is the woman he desires or idealizes.

THE MOON

Desire for Security

If a man's heart is a woman, mother Moon is his great nourisher. The food-giver. She owns the cookie jar. Her position in the sky at the moment of our birth shows where we seek security and nurturing . She reveals our relationship to our mother, our family, where we look to be protected and sustained, and our emotional response to others. The Moon is a man's heart and her solar field position shows the kind of woman he looks to for emotional nurturing.

If a man does not have a sense of being sustained in his heart (by his inner mother), if he is out of touch or cannot feel her (the Moon's) inner nurturing, then he will seek that nurturing in a woman. He will put the woman in a mother role, and if that woman is not strong, she will fall into the temptation of gaining power from the man's needs and "keep the man a boy." In this case, she is really in charge of the cookie jar.

> "...her ability to say "no" to him means that she has to say "no" also to her own indulgent tendencies and face her emotions, no matter of what nature they may be, without being swamped. This is said to be the lesser sacrifice, but it is no easy one to make. It involves the breaking of her identification with her son and the relinquishing of her position of superiority as giver."
> (*Woman's Mysteries Ancient and Modern* by M. Esther Harding.)

She must refuse to mother the man because this kind of relationship will prevent her from finding her natural male strength residing in her own heart. If this man's need seduces her into power and control, the relationship will eventually fail. Even though many couples stay together under such conditions, they live only a piece of life. They miss the fullness of an intimacy that is only possible between a true man and a true woman.

The Moon rules the stomach, home, family, real estate, and relates to emotional and material comfort. Her daily motion through the sky shows the general mood of the people on earth any given day. She is very important for predicting the outcome of an event or enterprise.

THE FIVE PERSONAL PLANETS IN THE 12 ENERGY FIELDS

THE MOON IN THE 12 SOLAR FIELDS

The Moon In The Aries Solar Field - Fire
KEY PHRASE:
"I gain security from starting new things, embracing new challenges, and I like being impulsive."

If your Moon is here, you gain your security and nurturing from new adventures. You love to try new things and to be with people who can make quick decisions. Since these are the energies that you were associated with from birth, they are the most comfortable for you. You may have trouble finishing things because it is more important for you to start them. You are a "doer" not a "finisher." But you can inspire others to take action by taking the lead yourself. You are attracted to strong and aggressive people who are not afraid to make things happen. You are not emotionally "mushy" and seldom look back. You are more interested in what is happening now or what lies ahead of you.

A man with his Moon here will love you if you are a fiery woman. The fiery fields of Aries, Leo, and Sagittarius are his primary emotional interests. Women with planets in these fields are very active and outgoing and he receives a lot of emotional support from their gifts of energy since his own internal woman is fire.

The Moon In The Taurus Solar Field - Earth
KEY PHRASE:
"I feel nurtured and sustained by plenty of money, good food, and great sex."

Taurus is a very solid earth energy. If your Moon is here you have a strong practical sense and are probably good at handling money. You love the good things of the earth. Usually you can cook well, create a garden, or build a structure. You need time and space to move around because you cannot be pushed into anything. It is best to coax you into something because you are more likely to respond to gentle nudging. You are fixed and stubborn but loyal in your feelings to your mate, home and family. You are also very sensuous and love to touch unless some other planetary pattern interferes with this. You find it hard to forsake your mate even if your relationship is not working.

If a mate has his Moon here, you will have a loyal husband. But make sure you have some Taurus, Virgo, or Capricorn (earth energies) or Cancer, Scorpio, or Pisces (water energies) in your nature, because these energies are the most compatible with his. Don't be surprised if he does not say that he loves you. He has a strong reluctance to verbalize how he feels. Of course, he may not know how he feels. Sometimes it will be like having to pry open a clam with a needle to get him to talk about what he is feeling. He usually expects you to know how he feels without him having to say anything. This seems to be due to the natural stubbornness of the Taurus nature. He loves a woman who is a good cook, good at sex, sensual, and loyal to the family. He is usually very predictable but loyal and steadfast. It is important to never push him or make any kind of demands. Ask and suggest is the best approach. Being vulnerable is not easy for him but he can show his love in many ways because he is loyal in his affections.

The Moon In The Gemini Solar Field - Air
KEY PHRASE:
> *"I feel nurtured by good books, great ideas, living in two places at once, and having lots of choices."*

Here the Moon is in an airy energy field which reveals restless and intellectual habits. There is always a need to be in two places at once, to do more than two things at a time, an impatience for detail, distaste for finishing long projects, and a tendency toward being emotionally indecisive. Here, the feelings tend to be in the head unless other planets are in water energies that express more emotions connected to the heart.

If your Moon is here, you seek comfort in new techniques, new methods, and change in your surroundings. You love the feeling of moving around and are attracted to change. You may even like to live or sleep in two places, going back and forth whenever you feel like it.

As we have learned, the Moon is always a very important planet when we are trying to understand a man's heart and emotion. Here his heart is in his head. He could be very fickle and have two love affairs going on at the same time. If you ask him which woman he likes the most, his answer may be, "I like both of them." If you press him to answer which one he loves, he may say, "I don't know. I will have to think about it." (The word "love" makes him very uncomfortable because it implies commitment.) He will have difficulty in being committed to one woman because his preferred choice is two. It is very difficult for this man to open his heart and become vulnerable because his need for options prevent him from taking that risk. He never wants to be in a position where he cannot turn back. He will be attracted to a Gemini woman because she reflects who he is — dualistic in nature — but both of them tend to "live in the head."

The Moon In The Cancer Solar Field - Water
KEY PHRASE:
"I feel nurtured by my home, my family, and money in the bank for a rainy day."

Here the Moon is in a water energy field which lends changing fluctuations to the emotions. There can be marked mood changes and sensitivity to the immediate environment. Since the Moon changes to a different energy field every two and a half days, a woman born with her Moon here seems to reflect these changes in attitude. There seems to be a deep attunement to the lunar cycle which reflects emotional withdrawal from others during the menstrual cycle. People with the Moon here tend to be moody.

If your Moon is here, you are a true homebody. You love the family, your hearth, and a cupboard full of goodies to feed those in need. You are sensitive to other people's feelings as well as your own. You could cry in a moment as emotions are full within you. You can be possessive and over-motherly to those who look to you as the great provider. Beware of playing the role of mother to the man. If it is your tendency to keep your husband dependent on you as his mother, you may end up with a boy instead of a man.

If a man has his Moon here, he is also strongly attached to the family and probably has a strong emotional connection to his mother. But it is very important that he has broken his apron strings, otherwise he will expect you to be like his mother. He may actually love playing the role of being a mother himself — taking care of the kids and cooking a good meal. The water energies of Scorpio and Pisces and the earth energies of Taurus, Virgo, and Capricorn go well with his Moon. If you have planets in these signs, his Moon would fit well with you. He will be sensitive and a good provider to the family, but make sure he doesn't expect you to be his mother. Eventually you would resent that.

The Moon In The Leo Solar Field - Fire
KEY PHRASE:
> "I feel nurtured by attention from others, love experiences, being creative, and expressing myself emotionally."

This fiery energy field gives an intense and dramatic expression to the Moon. There is usually a strong desire for romance, creativity, and the arts. If your Moon is here, you love to create an emotional impact on others while being at the center of attention. While others may avoid the limelight, you love to be at the center of the action. Of course this could be nullified if your Moon is "afflicted" by unfriendly planets. In general, you are very positive and can't stand moody or depressing people. In fact, you are usually the one who lifts other people's spirit because you always see hope and light where other people do not. You love expressing the energy of life and inspiring people to do their best. You have a deep love nature and enjoy the whole realm of romance. You could be strongly drawn to acting or music because these areas provide you with a channel for creative self-expression.

A man with his Moon here is looking for a woman with an Amazonian spirit. She is a fiery and ardent ideal for his heart. He is looking for a strong and self-assured woman who will match his romantic expectations. He could be a romantic Casanova because he may be attached to the drama of romance rather than the intensity of real love. He will talk a lot about the heart, but make sure the words match his exaggerations. If you are a fiery Leo, Sagittarius, or Aries woman, you would fit his emotional expectations. He usually loves sports and the spirit of competition as he longs to savor the sweet victory to match his aggressive and sometimes gigantic ego. But he does have a big heart and will be generous to the woman he loves. Are you his fiery goddess?

The Moon In The Virgo Solar Field - Earth
KEY PHRASE:
> *"I am nurtured and sustained by order, perfection, beauty and helping others."*

Here the Moon falls into a box where she is kept in a neat and tidy place. This is like the feelings that are kept under control due to an overt need to maintain order, efficiency, accuracy and perfection. The habits are particular, patient, and show great capacity for boring and tedious work. The Virgo Moon type can endure long hours of repetitive work as if they had a machine in the back of their brain that could go on forever. The problem with this is that the feelings are mentalized — not really felt. Romantic feelings may be considered "mush." Let us hope that other parts of the nature can balance off this passion for efficiency with passion for love.

If your Moon is in Virgo, you are probably loyal in love and reliable but you may have trouble knowing your feelings and expressing your emotions. You can be a very responsible and caring mother who knows how to carry out your duties effectively but actually you need to practice being foolish.

A man with his Moon here is usually critical of women. He expects his mate to really have her life together. If she does not, then he can be the worst fussbudget and critic around. In a sense his heart is in his head and he has a hard time losing himself emotionally. You may resent the fact that he has it so together. He takes himself too seriously and does not know how to be foolish. He needs to practice throwing his expectations out the window because they originate in his brain and not in his heart. He has to practice occasional mindlessness. Otherwise, he will not fall helpless in the heart when he falls in love. He will idealize you if you are a Virgo. But if you are not the efficient type, he could be your worst nagger. The water energies of Pisces, Cancer, Scorpio, and the earth energies of Taurus and Capricorn work best with him.

The Moon In The Libra Solar Field - Air
KEY PHRASE:
> "I am nurtured and sustained by harmonious surroundings, beautiful music, and loving friends."

Libra is an energy field of relationship and cooperation. If you have this Moon, you like to be with people and to be known as a person who is very friendly and helpful to others. People tend to like you because you know how to charm them and get them to like you. You are interested in the beautiful. A pleasant, colorful atmosphere in your home is very important to you and you seek harmony with everything you relate to. But there could be some tendency to use people to seek an advantage. If this is done, all your charm will fail you. So practice sincerity of feeling in all your relationships.

A man with his Moon here loves a pleasant, sensitive, and attractive woman. He is drawn to a refined woman who is usually connected to design, music, art, or public relations. He likes to expand his social boundaries. But he dislikes making definite decisions and may be hard to pin down. His habits of changing his viewpoints to accommodate the situation can be very disappointing if you are looking for more conviction. The Libra energy leads him to feel that a one-sided viewpoint is impossible. He is often driven to make no decision at all. If the planetary energies are favorable to his Moon, he can be a great negotiator and find points of agreement between people. He has a very pleasant side and he likes a woman who has these qualities. His woman is not a fiery go-getter. She is kind, social and probably very good looking. At least this is what he is looking for in his relationship to her. Although peace and harmony are his ideals, he can create conflicts by not taking a stand for what he feels because of a need for options.

The Moon In The Scorpio Solar Field - Water
KEY PHRASE:

> *"I am nurtured and sustained by a loyal lover, adventurous sex, and being in control of my world."*

Here the Moon is in a mysterious water field. What you see is not what you get. If your Moon is here, you are a "still water runs deep" person. Your inner life is not well known by others and you like to keep it that way. You are extremely sensitive to accusation or blame. No one should ever point their finger at you if they wish to remain your friend. Once you are hurt, you do not forgive easily and you may look for a way to get even. Your private life is very important to you. This is why you usually have many secrets. You like to probe into the causes of things and have a strong awareness of people's hidden motives. You could be a researcher, detective, psychologist or mystic. You are not easy to know. Therefore your greatest challenge will be to practice the willingness to be known, because this is the true way to intimacy.

A man with his Moon here is usually just as "clammed up" as the man with a Taurus Moon. He will almost never open up to what he is really feeling. Because of this tendency to control himself, he has usually lost touch with who he is emotionally and may not really know how he feels about anything. He will not consciously make a choice to open up. Life has to do it to him. Some event of great consequences must awaken his feelings. He will rarely even decide to do so. The kind of woman he is looking for is very sensual and sexual who loves to explore the depths of sexuality. However, if his heart is not awakened, his desires manifest themselves more as lust than as love. But this is his lesson: to learn the true difference between lust and love. If he does this, and you have Scorpio energies in your nature, he can be the greatest lover because he will share the depths of himself through true intimacy.

The Moon In The Sagittarius Solar Field - Fire
KEY PHRASE:
> "*I am nurtured by the outdoors, far away places, and the feeling of traveling.*"

This energy field imparts a fiery impulse to the emotions. There is a great interest in mobility. Traveling and wandering are very strong tendencies. There is also a strong need for adventure — to find out what is beyond the horizon, to connect with distant lands, people, and foreign cultures.

If your Moon is here, you love traveling and moving around. You could be very interested in spiritual matters, law, writing, publishing, and teaching. You are usually a very open person emotionally, uncomplicated, and forthright. You despise deception and could never keep a secret. Although you may not be conscious of it, you are seeking to understand the greater picture of your life. You are in search of meaning.

A man with his Moon here is looking for a free-spirited mate who is willing to "take off" at a moment's notice to explore what's over the mountain. He may be interested in motorcycles and want you to jump on for a ride. There is a strong need for mobility. If you like this lifestyle, then you fit with him. He will usually be very honest and you will always know where you stand with him. At times, he can be very blunt and unfeeling, but no harm is intended. It's just the way he is. He says how he sees it. If you are looking for a sensitive and subtle man, this one is not for you. He does not live in subtlety. His sexual needs appear to be mostly instinctual and he does not tend to take a long time at lovemaking. He is usually not the romantic type. He is an adventurer. If you have similar planetary energies (Sagittarius, Leo, or Aries) go for it. His lifestyle may wear you out, but it will never be boring.

The Moon In The Capricorn Solar Field - Earth
KEY PHRASE:
> "I am nurtured by my family, tradition, ancestors, and my standing in the world."

This lunar position gives a strong practical and pragmatic sense to the feelings. The feelings are not spontaneous. They are predictable because they function within the boundaries of what is the proper and correct thing to do. The feelings tend to be restricted to security and position in life.

If your Moon is here, you could have an ambitious side. You tend to be serious and carry that kind of mood with you. It is good to have other more bouncy and spontaneous energies to express in your other planets to prevent regular depression. If you don't have these other kinds of solar energies, you need to be around people who are lighthearted to keep up your spirits. You are usually a very responsible person and feel that duty is a very important principle to follow. You are usually honest and forthright about your feelings because you wear no illusions about your emotional self. This is why when your judgment is keen, it is often very good. All the fluff is removed from your expectations. You have a very practical and realistic outlook toward your world. Sentimentality is certainly not in your vocabulary.

A man with his Moon here will admire a woman of standing in the community. She is mature and somewhat reserved in her nature. He is attracted to the predictable and practical side of a Capricorn woman. He is somewhat cool emotionally and tends to take himself too seriously. He is attracted to a woman who wants to build things together. Home, business and family tradition are very meaningful words to him and he wants to build on them. The world as it is looks very real to him. Perhaps that is why he gets moody and depressed at times. Only the practical, the ambitious, and the sensible woman qualifies for him. He may also find comfort in the other earthy qualities of Taurus and Virgo and would probably work well with them.

The Moon In The Aquarius Solar Field - Air
KEY PHRASE:
> "I am nurtured by my friends, new experiences, and the unexpected."

This energy field is full of surprises, brilliance and the unusual. If your Moon is here, your emotions have a marked difference from the rest of your nature — unless, of course, you have a lot of other planets in this energy field. This is a radical energy and quite unpredictable. Therefore, your emotional reactions will always surprise people — even yourself. You could be fascinated by unusual relationships with other people and have a strong need to be independent and totally free to do your own thing. You may unconsciously choose people who are married or not attached to anyone so that your own freedom is guaranteed. Don't be surprised that few people really understand you. Your reactions are just not predictable, even to yourself. You do recognize the rights of others to be free and certainly demand that for yourself. You tend to live on the edge of experience, always open to new influences if they offer you the opportunity to grow. Your friends may claim that you are too detached emotionally; that you don't seem connected emotionally to others; and that you always seem to maintain an unreachable distance from them.

A man with his Moon here loves to have a lot of women friends. If you expect more loyalty or affection from your mate, you could have a hard time with this man. He may not be involved sexually with other women but he certainly wants to keep his options open. He may be very experimental sexually, sometimes even on the kinky side. He can seem to be unreachable at times because he is not usually connected to his feelings. He could be looking at other women while he is with you. If this offends you, then he is definitely not for you. If you don't also have an uncommitted and detached nature, this man could drive you to rage with his indifference. He, like the Gemini Moon type, has to have his heart opened so deeply that love breaks through his resistance to true intimacy. Eventually, he has to learn that real love is not bondage — that it actually brings freedom. Of course, everyone needs to learn this, but the man with an Aquarian Moon needs it most of all because he lives in a cold and windy place that is rarely visited by the Sun.

The Moon In The Pisces Solar Field - Water
KEY PHRASE:
> *"I am nurtured by caring for others, escaping into my dreams, and finding peak experiences that fit my inspirations."*

Here the Moon wanders in the world of imagination, feeling, fantasy, dreams, and tears. If your Moon is in this watery field, you are full of feeling. Where other people may fall short in emotions, you are overflowing. You can be moved quickly to tears because you are in tune with the suffering of the world. You may even have a deep sense of sorrow or loss without knowing why and try to squash your own need to help fulfill the needs of others. You have a great capacity to love but the danger may lie in not feeling enough for yourself. Your needs and self-nurturing are also important, but it may take you some time to accept this. So care must be taken to not overdo your empathy for others. You could drain your energy and be used and abused by others if you don't draw the line on this side of safety. You have a far-reaching imagination and the power to create an effect or illusion. You could act, dance, or write. The best way to use your intuitive and psychic talents are in the arts. Avoid alcohol or mind-expanding stimulants because you could open psychic doors that would be hard to close. If you have a need to escape this "cruel world," then do so through creative self-expression.

When a man has his Moon here, he is looking for a sensitive and emotionally deep woman. Since he is a very sympathetic and sensitive person, he looks for these qualities in his woman. He sees her as beautiful, sensual, and capable of supporting his dreams. He is an idealist, but he may suffer times of deep melancholy or depression and seek escape through drugs, alcohol, or other self-destructive habits. He may be emotionally weak because life can feel like an uphill battle for him. However, he does have great capacity to care and love. If he is awakened at the heart, his love could be deeper than all the other men you have known. He may have trouble dealing with the real world, but if his heart is alive, he could be a great musician, writer, or actor. The water energies of Cancer and Scorpio and the earth energies of Capricorn, Taurus, and Virgo go best with him. When involved with this kind of man always ask, "Does he see the real me, or is he experiencing me as an illusion of his own imagination?"

VENUS AND MARS

Just as the Sun and Moon relate to the father and mother, strength and nurturing (the heart of the woman and the heart of the man), Venus and Mars relate to our feminine and masculine sexuality. While both man and woman have Venus and Mars energies in their nature, these energies are expressed differently in a masculine and feminine body.

Being physically a female, a woman identifies with her Moon and Venus nature, but she is seeking that other part of herself, the Sun and Mars, in the outside world which is reflected in the form of a man. Her discovery is to finally realize that the outer man she is attracted to is herself — her very own heart and passion. When she discovers how to become totally intimate with this outside male, she will discover that she has become totally intimate with herself. She will come to know and love who she is as a woman, no longer at war with the masculine god of her own heart. She will feel her own inner strength. This is the heart-awakened woman.

Obviously, as described by my own experience in the early part of this book, the same process holds true for a man, but in reverse. That is, being physically a male, he identifies with his Sun and Mars, but seeks that other part of himself, the Moon and Venus, in the form of a woman. When he has awakened the lunar goddess within himself by giving his heart totally to a woman in the outside world, he comes home to his own heart. He feels nurtured and sustained within and knows who he is emotionally. He is the heart-awakened man.

VENUS

Desire to Receive Love and To Share Feelings

It is important to realize that Venus is also a planet of value. She shows what we like, our friends, our preferred relationships, our refinement and those people we want around us. She is very important in showing us how we feel about ourselves.

As a planet of value, Venus rules money and the sense of self-worth in the lives of both men and women. If she is afflicted from birth (hindered by Saturn, Neptune, or Pluto), we will have difficulty liking and caring for ourselves and tend to give in to the needs of others because we don't value ourselves or know what we feel or need. In this case, we simply cannot stand up for something we do not feel to be true.

Whether it is a woman's Venus or a man's Venus, she is a planet that shows our desire and need to receive love. Venus is the desire to be appreciated and to receive strokes from our friends, family, lover, beauty, and the arts. It also relates to sexuality because it seeks intimacy with the lover. This seeking may be motivated by sheer lust or divine ecstasy. The kind of pleasure we receive through Venus depends on our capacity to love and to be truly intimate without fear. Venus is one of the keys to a man's heart because it shows the kind of woman he sees as his ideal. The solar field his Venus is in at birth gives us this all-important key.

The solar field that your Venus is in at birth describes your attitude towards those things you love and appreciate. It shows the type of people you prefer to have in your life, the kind of pleasures you seek and the type of person you prefer for sharing sex and intimacy. Venus is the key to understanding the relationships you have in every human experience. Its primary urges are pleasure, love, and ecstasy.

VENUS IN THE 12 SOLAR FIELDS

Venus In The Aries Solar Field - Fire
KEY PHRASE:
> *"I love starting new things, challenges, fiery friends, and lovers."*

When Venus is found here, her gentle and kind nature turns more into a warring spirit. Venus is not at home here. She will test her friends and lovers with a competitive attitude. If your Venus is here, then you love a challenge and the test of wills. You simply enjoy the forceful energy and sparks that arise from engaging a challenger in a relationship. This energy brings out the tigress in you. You are attracted to men who are strong and energetic or friends and women of like nature. You tend to like competitive sports that whet your appetite for winning. This position of Venus could be called the "feminine warrior." Love seems to turn into a game of conquest and sexuality seems to be boundless. The sexual embrace tends to be expressed without reserve or reluctance. In short, this position of Venus makes you an aggressive lover. Some men may be threatened by that but certainly not those who have their Sun in Aries, Leo, or Sagittarius. These three fields are very fiery and love the energy exchange with a woman who has Venus in Aries. Check to see if your Venus is "afflicted" by other planets. If so, you would have a difficult time fulfilling your desires because of a poor self-image or fear of intimacy.

Venus In The Taurus Solar Field - Earth
KEY PHRASE:
> "I love plenty of money, sensual people, quality restaurants, and a loyal lover."

Venus here is very sensual, earthy, loyal and predictable. If you find a man with his Venus in Taurus, he will love good food, probably be a good cook, work hard to make money (he loves money), and love a woman who is usually big-boned or has lots of body. He does not like skinny women. Like the Taurus woman, he is very sensual and loves to touch. He does have a couch-potato side and is slow in his actions. He likes to lay around and may be somewhat lethargic, but he has very endearing qualities. He is very reliable and true in his affections toward his mate, just as a woman would be if she had Venus in Taurus or Sun in Taurus. He may not say he loves you but assumes you know it. The important thing here is that you know whether you are his kind of woman. A man has a tendency to see his woman through the eyes of Venus, even though she may not be that type at all. (In this case, a

Taurus type.) If you don't fit his Venus image, your relationship will soon run into trouble because you will get tired of trying to be a Taurus woman when you are not. Once he opens up to you, it will be hard for him to let you go as he is very tenacious in his feelings. These kind of men in general have a difficult time saying goodbye or walking away. Of course, if you have Venus in Taurus, you will like a Taurus man and he will like what you like. If your Sun is in Taurus, then this kind of man would love to be with you because you are his ideal; your Sun reflects his Venus.

Venus In The Gemini Solar Field - Air

KEY PHRASE:
> *"I love to have two lovers, smart friends, beautiful words, and great ideas."*

You love knowledge, ideas, techniques, methods, books, colored pens, and many friends. Because of this, you could be a poet, reporter, or writer. Music also appeals to your artistic nature. You are attracted to men who are smart, witty, and clever. A great idea can sometimes affect you deeply. You have a love for doing two things at once. Beware of the man who has his Venus in Gemini. He could be a flirt, inconsistent, and deceptive. He usually has one or two women on a string. The important word here is "two." Like you, (if your Venus is here) he likes to do two things at once. Only in his case, it is being with two women. Venus is usually a warm and charming planet, but here she takes on more of a mental expression. A man with his Venus here is strongly attracted to a Gemini woman. His ideal woman is a pixy, with a somewhat androgynous body type, who lives more in her head than in her body. He, like you, (if you are a Gemini or have Venus in Gemini) has a certain need to be free and uncommitted because who knows what opportunity may be waiting around the corner. If you want to be free to explore relationship and don't care about commitment, then this man can be a match for you. But to grow emotionally and discover the real freedom you are looking for, you will need to engage in true intimacy from the heart and forget your head.

Venus In The Cancer Solar Field - Water
KEY PHRASE:
> "I love feeding others, being their mother, nurturing their needs, and having a comfortable home."

This position of Venus imparts the love of home and family. The glowing fireplace with family members gathered around with an abundant supply of food is a scene you are attracted to. The solar field of Cancer rules the stomach. Therefore you could be very attracted to the culinary arts. Great chefs will often have their Venus in Cancer. There seems to be a great pleasure gained from feeding everyone well. Home and security are extremely important to you. You are also quiet sensitive to the atmosphere around you and you have very deep emotions. You tend to have some strong maternal tendencies and will often find yourself in that role. If you run into a man who has his Venus here, he will expect you to do his laundry, bake his cookies, bring him drinks, and be a good mother. He will also be strongly attached to the home and family. He is usually a good family man. He loves children and wants to sustain the family tradition and values. The danger may be that he expects you to replace his mother emotionally. This could put a real burden on you, because he may not yet be a man. He could see you as the one who is supposed to nurture him and take care of his needs. Beware of the temptation to keep this man a boy.

Venus In The Leo Solar Field - Fire
KEY PHRASE:
> "I love romance, expressing my heart, chasing love, and creating an emotional impact on others."

Here, Venus softens the heart. The fiery field of Leo is the natural expression of the heart. Leo is the energy field of romance, children, and creativity. With your Venus here, you tend to be in love with love. You could also be in love with the arts, for you are drawn to anything that will enable you to express love on a deeper level. You may be drawn to music and drama. A man with his Venus here will be attracted to a woman who is fiery, spontaneous, energetic, and very outgoing. He likes drama and is drawn to a woman who is warm and expressive. He can be very romantic and attentive to the things that make a woman happy. His ideal is a Leo woman but another fiery sign will do — Aries or Sagittarius. He also loves sports and the challenge of conquest. He is something of a lion in search of a throne. He is proud yet easily hurt if rejected. He looks at money as a tool for enjoying life and usually has a very generous heart. If you have these same attitudes, he could be your mate. Find out if you have any relationship planets (Sun, Mars, Moon or Venus) in Leo or if any of the bigger planets are related to his Venus by conjunction.

Venus In The Virgo Solar Field - Earth
KEY PHRASE:
> "I love to create order, beauty, and to stay in touch with the earth. I love to help those who need me."

The attitudes of Virgo are to be efficient, to organize information and keep life together. Virgos place a great deal of value on service and a job well done. If your Venus is found here, you certainly value these traits. The one problem with this is that Virgo is basically very mental in its function. The energy is turned more toward the mind and its capacity to work well, rather than toward feeling or the heart. A Venus in Virgo person is in love with a great plan, a fine work of art, or a beautiful design. The pure expression of love may seem a little mushy for her. She feels that duty and service are much more valuable than a temporary romance. When a man has his Venus here he tends to be very critical of women and very particular and fussy in his habits. He loves a very neat lady who has herself together and who is very organized. As you can see, these attitudes are not about love. They are about qualifications. Does the woman measure up to his standards? The only woman who could measure up would probably be a woman who has her Sun in Virgo. To the Virgo, order and efficiency are the lords of life, not the heart.

Venus In The Libra Solar Field - Air
KEY PHRASE:
> "I love color, music, art, beauty, harmony, and being accepted by my friends."

Venus is a happy planet here because she loves relationship and here she is in the solar field of relationship. Libra is the realm of togetherness, bringing opposites into harmony. Venus is very harmonious here. She responds to beautiful music, great colors, and peaceful surroundings. If you have Venus here, you will be drawn to beauty in many forms — beautiful friends, beautiful sounds, and a beautiful love. The attitudes of Libra are full of options and alternatives. Therefore anyone with Venus in this field likes to have many friends and many choices. This is why it is difficult to get this Libra type to take a stand for something: they like to keep their options open. Venus in Libra will seek a social advantage through her charm and play the butterfly game — going from relationship to relationship in search of her ideal. This is positive if she is pursuing love from the heart, but detrimental if she is merely seeking a strategic love advantage and not allowing herself to be vulnerable. A man with Venus here is looking for a soft and charming lady who is very cooperative and pliable. He, too, loves friends — especially women. He can be charming but beware of vacillation in his feelings and his lack of commitment. If your Venus is here, you both could do well in the arts but indecisiveness could overwhelm you.

Venus In The Scorpio Solar Field - Water
KEY PHRASE:
"I love the mystery of sex, the joy of intensity, loyalty in love, and being with one person."

Here Venus is intrigued by sex and mystery. She loves to explore the inner workings of a relationship on every level. However, Scorpios have a tendency to conceal. There is a great reluctance to being known. Venus here hides her feelings until she knows it is safe or can stay in charge. Her primary goal is control, to avoid being vulnerable at all costs, but this is truly a mistake because she has a great capacity to engage a relationship on the deepest level. Her greatest lesson is to discover true intimacy; to turn her heart over to another.

If your Venus is here, you are a cautious lover. Therefore, you can appear to be something you are not to others. This is usually because they do not know you. You will need to abandon your control and engage your lover on a very vulnerable level. Then you will have a channel to express your depths. A man with his Venus here is fiercely loyal, but usually reserved emotionally. He is very sexual and is attracted to intense and mysterious looking women. You may find it hard to get him to "open up." At times, it will seem impossible. He is very reluctant to say how he feels, but he may not know how he feels, or may fear the consequences of opening up. He is a silent pursuer. He can be a good sex partner but will have a hard time being vulnerable. If he is not opening his heart, he is probably more interested in lust than in love.

Venus In The Sagittarius Solar Field - Fire
KEY PHRASE:
> "I love the outdoors, wide open spaces, knowledge, foreign countries, traveling, horses, and the truth."

This fiery field imparts the love for adventure, distant contacts, spiritual truths, publishing, law, writing, and foreign countries. If your Venus is here, you are attracted to far away places and foreign cultures. You like a man who is straightforward, honest, and who tells it like it is. You have a love for truth and an aversion for deception and trickery. It is hard for you to keep a secret and you may blurt out confidential information on impulse. You don't like to gather any moss. You love the outdoors and the challenge of new experiences. The adventures of travel and the contacts you make with people from a foreign country who represent a different culture can be of special interest to you. A man with his Venus here is attracted to a woman with the Amazonian spirit. He, too, loves a woman who is outspoken and freedom loving. He will want to take her on new adventures and explore new challenges together. He sees his woman as an adventurous partner always on the go and ready to explore the next experience over the horizon. If you are not this type, don't expect him to be around very long. He does not tend to be very sensitive or hold on to the past. Sentimentality is not his style. He does not look back.

Venus In The Capricorn Solar Field - Earth
KEY PHRASE:
> "I love the tried, the true, and the predictable. I love the past, older friends, and what went before me."

The earthy field of Capricorn imparts a very practical and pragmatic attitude. It tends to limit itself to the physical world and avoids the subtle. It is very interested in matters at hand. If your Venus is here, you love tradition, organization, position, prestige, and status. You are ambitious to find a place in the world, a place of leadership and responsibility. You look more toward what worked before and want to continue doing the same thing. Some of your friends might say you are "a stick in the mud," implying that you rarely venture beyond the predictable. You love order, efficiency, and like to be in charge of large enterprises. You like people who have achieved a position in society and you are attracted to conventional occupations: real estate, law (for status, power, and control), medicine, or science. You will probably marry an older man. A man with his Venus here loves a woman of tradition. He honors the family and sees himself as the leader of the clan. He is attracted to a Capricorn woman who is his ideal. His ideal woman is sensible, organized, practical, and responsible. He is not very expressive emotionally. Duty is more important to him than emotions. He wants a good wife who will raise his family well. He honors the conventional woman who is predictable and reliable and who wants to build a life together — preferably a family empire.

Venus In The Aquarius Solar Field - Air
KEY PHRASE:
> *"I love my friends, the unusual, the hard to get, and sexual freedom."*

Watch out for this guy. If your mate has his Venus here, he loves his freedom to explore other options. Although he is not as indecisive as Gemini or Libra (the two other airy fields), he is just as noncommittal. He loves women, but it is hard for him to stay and love only one. If you find yourself in an intimate relationship with him, you have to understand that you could be one of the many. He is not loyal in his affections to one woman because he always needs options to choose another. He may not be promiscuous but you could swear he is. He doesn't see anything wrong with having many different women friends — even as different lovers at the same time. If you are looking for a predictable and committed love life, walk in the opposite direction. You won't find it here. On the other hand, if you are an Aquarian or have Venus here, you can understand him perfectly. You both will be free without attachments. The problem with this is that there is not much true heart energy. It is mostly experimentation and lust. He loves new technology, new friends, new ideas, and kinky sex. He is usually very creative, but don't ever expect him to be wherever you expect him to be. You will always be surprised, because he never knows what he will be doing tomorrow.

Venus In The Pisces Solar Field - Water

KEY PHRASE:

> "I love the other world, the unknown, sensitive people, and beautiful things. I have to help those people who need my help."

If you are looking for a very sensitive man, this one is it. If his Venus is here, he is very romantic, idealistic, imaginative, and probably very artistic. He is very caring and helpful to others and those in need. At least this is the nature of his Venus in her pure form, but he may have other planets which offset these idealistic attitudes. He is looking for a woman who is very emotional and expressive. She is deep, mysterious, and other-worldly. He is attracted to spiritual, artistic, or psychic types. He may have a strong desire to escape into a fantasy world or pursue stimulants to take him there — drugs or alcohol. The escape tendency is very strong but it can be expressed in a positive way if he is creative and responsible. If you have Venus here, you may be in pursuit of a dream or believe a relationship is something it is not. Beware of being in love with helping a man who is a "wounded bird." If you try to heal him, he will only fly away when he gets well. If you are something of a dreamer, artistic, or spiritual, he will probably love you for it and will always be there for you emotionally. He can be vulnerable and expressive. The drawback is that he may weep on your shoulders. Can you handle this?

MARS

The Desire to Take Action

Mars shows a man's aggressive energy. His obvious passion. What he goes after or pursues. His male sexuality. Mars shows the kind of man a woman desires sexually. Mars is an aggressive energy in both sexes. It is the desire to take action. It is a forward moving energy but expressed differently. When we consider Mars, we always have to take Venus into account, because she is the other side of sexuality.

In a man, Mars shows his sexual behavior towards Venus, the woman he is attracted to and idealizes. He desires to sexually penetrate the woman who relates to his Venus. If his Venus is in Scorpio and you are a Scorpio type of woman, you are the woman he desires. If your Mars, Sun, or Moon are in Scorpio, he could be strongly attracted to you sexually. We always have to keep in mind that Mars and Venus are very sexual planets. When the heart is open in love, these sexual energies can bring transcendental experiences of true intimacy.

The solar energy field your Mars is in at birth shows your aggressive desires and the masculine side of your sexuality. In a woman, it shows the kind of man she desires sexually. In a man, it shows his sexual desire when aroused by Venus.

Venus stimulates a man's Mars to sexual activity; shows him the kind of woman he desires sexually: the pleasures he enjoys; and what kind of woman he idealizes. Venus shows a woman her feminine nature and the pleasures she enjoys.

Mars is basically an outward-acting planet and Venus is basically an inner-acting planet. Venus is directed toward receiving love through the senses. Together, Mars and Venus rule and stimulate the sexual centers and magnetize men and women toward each other. When these planetary energies are linked to the open heart in both sexes (Sun and Moon), they can express the deepest possible intimacy between a man and a woman.

MARS IN THE 12 SOLAR FIELDS

Mars In The Aries Solar Field - Fire
KEY PHRASE:
"*I desire to be first in all my actions. I love a challenge and am energized by competition.*"

Mars is very much at home in this energy field and is very aggressive and impulsive. Sex is often seen as a challenge and a chase.

If you have this Mars, you have an aggressive side. You are good at starting things but not outstanding in finishing them. As a woman, you are attracted to strong and fiery men sexually and would enjoy playful encounters in the bedroom. If the man you are with is not as strong as you, you may not have much respect for him. You need someone who can match your energy. You are an adventurer and you look to the man who has a fiery and active nature who will challenge you. The man you are interested in is a "doer", an initiator, one who is willing to take chances and take action in the moment. Since you are somewhat impulsive yourself, you are attracted to a man of a similar temperament. If your Mars is favorably connected to his Sun or Venus, this could be a very strong attraction. In fact, if your Mars is conjunct his Venus, the attraction can be so strong that it could be embarrassing. You are attracted to Aries, Leo, or Sagittarius men. These kind of men are fiery in nature which goes well with your own fiery side. Since air feeds fire, you are also attracted to the air signs of Gemini, Libra, and Aquarius.

Mars In The Taurus Solar Field - Earth
KEY PHRASE:
> *"Even though I am slow and steadfast in my actions, I am also tenacious, persistent, and loyal. I am in pursuit of material comfort."*

Mars in this solar energy field increases the pursuit for material gain. The passion is directed toward money, food, security, and acquisitions. Since Taurus expresses all the good things of the Earth, money, food, and sex, Mars here simply energizes all these needs.

If your Mars is here, your strongest sexual attraction is toward a Taurus man. If his Venus and your Mars are in this energy field, the passion can be very intense. You love the Taurus man's sensuality. He's usually into touching and very sexual. He has a very strong mating instinct, and you could be drawn to the intensity of his feelings. Although he is reluctant to verbalize his feelings due to an inherent stubbornness, you understand this because you are very much the same way. He expects his actions to reveal his love for you. He will show it in many ways. That's probably okay with you because you have the same tendency. If you find a Taurus in your life or a man with a lot of Taurus energies (planets in the Taurus energy field) a relationship will tend to last. Even if you eventually have trouble, it will be hard to break the bond between you. Neither one of you wants to say goodbye, so you may just have to let your relationship grind down over time if it is not working. Sooner or later, one of you will walk away. It is usually the woman.

Mars In The Gemini Solar Field - Air

KEY PHRASE:

> "I am restless. I have a million things going on and hate to finish them. I love starting new projects and exploring a dozen at a time."

Here Mars lends its energy to the mind. It gives an intense desire for knowledge, new ideas, techniques, methods, and communication. This is an airy, mental energy which does not seem connected to the body.

If your Mars is here, you are attracted to a Gemini man who is usually lost in thought and has his head in the heavens. This energy field also imparts the need to have an ongoing interest in two men at once. This may be embarrassing at first to admit because having two men at once certainly can complicate your life. The Gemini's tendency leads you to believe that if you make a choice for one you will miss out on the other. By always trying to keep your options open for another man, you could end up with nothing. But you find it hard to surrender your heart to one man.

You love a bright, sunny man who is full of new ideas and light energy. He is usually very intellectual, witty, clever, and changeable. You identify with this because this is part of your own nature. You seem to analyze sex a lot as if it were separate from your body. Since the Gemini Mars is not connected much to real feeling, your relationship may not last. You will feel that something is missing and that something is usually a lack of depth in feeling.

When someone asks you, "Do you love this guy?", your usual reply is "I think I do." Then you should ask yourself this: "What does thinking have to do with love?" If you love someone, do you only think you do?

Mars In The Cancer Solar Field - Water

KEY PHRASE:

> "I am in pursuit of security, home, family and nurturing. I like to make a nest and store my possessions there."

This energy field ignites Mars to go after security — to maintain the home, country, and flag. He is in search of security for his home and family.

If you like the hearth and Cancer energy is part of your intimacy planets, then this could be your man. Like you, if your Mars is here, this man is very emotional. He likes to express his feelings and shows great sympathy for his children and small things that need his help. Since you want a family man who shows his feelings, this one could be for you. Your home environment has to be safe and secure before you feel like being intimate. You have a shy side when it comes to sex, but if you are sure everything is safe around you, you can be the best of lovers. You know feelings and how to express them. Things of the past which were full of family enjoyment touch you deeply and you identify strongly with a man who feels the same. A Mars in Cancer man has a lot of the boy in him. If home and hearth are not your path, this man could annoy you with his fluctuating emotions and sentiment for little things. It is wise to choose that man who flows with your own emotional depths. You would also find attraction to the other water energies of Pisces and Scorpio and the earth energies of Virgo and Capricorn.

Mars In The Leo Solar Field - Fire
KEY PHRASE:
> "I am in pursuit of love and romance. I love the adventure of love and creativity. I seek the center stage and like to be in charge of my affairs."

Mars in Leo is in pursuit of love, creativity, and the emotional adventure. Here he is the actor who desires center stage. He never wants to be last in anything. He always wants to be first. He soaks up attention and praise and can be easily flattered. He is proud, strong, and full of self.

If your Mars is here, you are attracted to a lionhearted type of man who has a big heart, always full of possibility, who has a strong dislike for negative and dark egos. You love his spirit and the strength he radiates because he reflects your own desire to find the center of life — your passion for recognition and achievement. A man with his Sun in Leo can awaken your Martian desire for intimacy. The radiance of his presence stimulates the Mars energy field of love, passion, romance, and thrill. You are energized by his energy. There is a great magnetic attraction which stimulates your desire for him.

The other energy fields of Aries and Sagittarius would also appeal to you because they impart the fiery energy that stimulates your own Mars which express the energy of Leo. You would also find harmonious lovemaking with the solar fields of Gemini, Libra, and Aquarius because these are the airy energies that fan the fire of Leo's desire.

Mars In The Virgo Solar Field - Earth
KEY PHRASE:
> *"I am passionate for perfection. I pursue order, efficiency, and like to help others. I dislike anything coarse."*

The Virgo energy field imparts a very practical life function. The best in performance is required, demanded, and expected. Order and perfection are the primary impulses of this energy. When Mars is here, it simply gives a "passion for detail," efficiency, and doing one's best. Something organized and neat may give a greater thrill than an orgasm.

If your Mars is here, you are in pursuit of a man who is neat, organized, clean and efficient. Your passion tends to be in your head. Order and efficiency comes first, then passion. You probably could not stand making love in a sloppy bed. You could be a loyal and dutiful wife but may have to take occasional foolish risks. Being so together all the time can keep you in a rut. The border of the heart must be pushed into the realms of wildness; the realm where your mind has surrendered to the body's desire. Still, you are capable of lasting love and are attracted to a man who has his life together. You will be strongly attracted to a Virgo man but a Taurus could provide the balance in passion that you need. He is practical yet very sensuous. You need that kind of intimacy to keep your body loose and your desires out of your head.

Mars In The Libra Energy Field - Air

KEY PHRASE:
> *"I am in pursuit of togetherness, personal harmony and beauty in all relationships."*

Since Libra is an energy field that imparts a desire for beauty, harmony, and idealism in relationship, Mars lends his passion to these tendencies.

If your Mars is here, you are in pursuit of harmony in relationship. But, sometimes, because of a desire for an idealized mate, your relationship may not be the one you imagine. Libra imparts such a strong need for harmony that the actual relationship may not be this way at all. Libra can give you the tendency to try and make a relationship fit your idealism — when, in fact, it does not. You could be indecisive when it comes to taking a stand for what you truly need. You can be a master at rationalization. For example, a friend might say that your husband doesn't give you enough attention, and you might reply, "But he does other things that are really great. He's a hard worker and gives me security." While this may be true, are you willing to sacrifice security for true intimacy? Sometimes your desire for harmony can be so great that you could pretend that it exists when it does not.

You want a man who seeks harmony in relationship. Therefore, you are strongly attracted to a Libra type. Try to find out where his other planets are, because you don't want to get an abundance of Libra planets. He would be plagued with more indecision than you. With the right balance of idealism and reality you can have a very satisfying intimacy. The fire signs of Aries, Leo and Sagittarius would be very helpful in keeping you from getting stalled with indecision and inspire you to share the many sides of your talent for harmony.

Mars In The Scorpio Energy Field - Water
KEY PHRASE:
> *"I am in pursuit of absolute union with another. I am intensely passionate, possessive, protective, and very sensitive to other people aggressions."*

This is the element of frozen water and Scorpio tends to fix the feelings in the unconscious. This field imparts intensity of feeling and desire. There is a strong need for an intense relationship that transcends the ordinary. When Mars is found here it adds emotion and sexual intensity to an energy that already expresses this.

If your Mars is here, you are in pursuit of a very intense relationship. You are seeking the depths of intimacy. But sometimes there is a secrecy about your desires because you may be somewhat embarrassed by them. You may not be comfortable with letting other people know how sexual you really are. But, since sexuality is one of your primary interests, you might as well get comfortable with it. There is no greater lover if your desires are linked to a loving heart. The problem may be that lust is greater than love. In this case, sex becomes the goal rather than love. There may be a certain reluctance to turn your heart over to another because you always want to maintain control. You seem to seek a position of safety from too much caring. After all, who wants to give her whole heart to another? No telling what that man will do with it. You may actually lose your heart! At some point, you will need to cross the line, be willing to be known, and share your complete depths with another. You have a capacity for great intimacy, once you give your heart to another.

The man you are looking for is obviously an intense Scorpio. He may be the quiet type but you can feel the intensity of energy between you without a word being said. He may not be very adept at saying how he feels. But he may be reflecting your own reluctance. Your challenge together will be in letting each other know how you really feel. After all, if anyone understands the depth of your desires, it is this one. The other energy fields of Cancer, Pisces, and Taurus are also in harmony with your needs.

Mars In The Sagittarius Energy Field - Fire
KEY PHRASE:
> "I am in pursuit of meaning and understanding. I will go a long way to find the truth. I have great passion for traveling and discovery."

Like Aries and Leo, this is another fiery energy field. It imparts wanderlust to the nature. There is a passion for travel, foreign countries, cross-country adventures, camping out, and exploring the unknown.

If your Mars is here, you could have a passion for far away places and always need time to take off on a trip. This position sometimes expresses the desire to pursue spiritual matters. Your father, or someone in your family, may be interested in these things. You see your self as a restless go-getter in search of answers. In some people this energy manifests primarily as a restless quality. You may be someone who gathers no moss. Certainly you rarely look back because you are interested only in the now and the future. When aroused, you have a fighting spirit but you are not necessarily a warrior. You certainly can be a hard worker. You prefer the outdoors and seek out other people of like mood.

The man you are looking for matches your desires. He is straightforward, honest, and adventurous. He will not only go where you want to go, he will add challenge and interest to your life. As a lover, he is not the tender type, but he has a lot of energy which can add to your own. Together you can create a real fire. The Sagittarius man fits your passion the best. But Aries and Leo men are also harmonious with your nature.

Mars In The Capricorn Energy Field - Earth
KEY PHRASE:
> "I am in pursuit of leadership, being in charge and reaching the top. I love a challenge. I believe only in the pragmatic."

The ancient observers have said that this field is like a goat. Goats "go-at" things and people and this fits the Capricorn instinct. This is an energy field of ambition, achievement, and need to reach the top. They love the old, the tried and the true, and are not usually interested in things beyond this world. They function primarily with the material. They are very practical people.

If your Mars is here, you have a strong drive to reach a position of control and leadership. You like to be in front and are willing to take a lot of responsibility if it is to your advantage. You have a passion for organization, efficiency, and control. You like to spend your energy moving things or making them happen. You much prefer pulling the strings rather than having others pull yours; and people tend to let you do that because your actions tend to back up your words.

You are attracted to a man who is ambitious, confident and reliable. He must be very responsible and honor tradition. You like the idea of teamwork and want to share your goals with him. You are inspired by his fatherly, wise nature and his head for business and leadership. The passion of Capricorn is not a wild and fiery thing, but it is reliable, enduring, and steadfast. It is dependable, never foolish or out of control. Obviously a Capricorn man fits your desire the best but you would also be attracted to Taurus and Virgo as they also have practical, earthy qualities that support your need for the predictable.

Mars In The Aquarius Energy Field - Air
KEY PHRASE:
> "I desire independence, sexual freedom, and the right to explore."

Here, Mars supports the need to be unpredictable. This energy is almost the reverse of Capricorn. This field imparts the need to explore the unknown, extend the boundaries of the mind and all relationships. It is highly experimental. This is perhaps the most independent of all the solar energy fields.

If your Mars is here, you have a passion for the unusual. You love to have many men friends and keep your options open to all possibilities. You like unusual men who can be eccentric, unpredictable and hard to figure out. You are always challenged and fascinated by the unreachable. It is as if you are only attracted to a man if you can't have him. This is why you may tend to get involved in complicated relationships. You could have affairs with married men who are only available for short periods of time. This way you are guaranteed your freedom. You may be unable to commit your heart totally to any one person because you are already married to the god of freedom. You seem to equate true intimacy with a kind of bondage. You like to explore many kinds of sexual relationships and think nothing of having more than two men in your life at the same time. Loyalty of affection is not something you feel deeply.

You are attracted to the Aquarian man, because he fits your need for the unpredictable. He lives on the edge of experience and you are drawn to these possibilities. There can be a lot of sexual thrills but you need to ask if this has anything to do with love. You may one day discover that real intimacy can bring you freedom. It does not take it away.

Mars In The Pisces Energy Field - Water
KEY PHRASE

"I am in pursuit of my dreams, ecstasy, and the world of imagination."

Pisces is the energy field of the sea of space and the ocean of the earth. It imparts a vast and nebulous feeling to the psyche and a longing to return to the source. It is a mystical and undefined energy that rules the unconscious realms of our mind.

If your Mars is here, you are in pursuit of a dream man. You are attracted to a sensitive man who is full of feeling and who may need your help. Feelings can run very deep between you and there can be a great capacity for intimacy. You may be drawn to the artistic, the psychic, and the creative part of a man. But beware of your tendency to attract men who rely upon you too much for support. There is something of the "savior" in you because you have an unconscious feeling of obligation to save others. Make sure that you don't become a sacrifice in the process. Avoid men who are into drugs or alcohol for these men fear life and cannot give you the support you need. Since commitment and intimacy require a clear and steady heart, this man may fall short. He may be in pursuit of a dream and follow his illusion so strongly that he is out of touch with reality. Your passion is deep and full of great feeling but be careful of the men you attract into your life. Avoid weak and wounded men who look for you to save them. They will sap all of your energy.

You are strongly attracted to the Pisces man, but men with planets in the energy fields of Cancer and Scorpio can also share the emotional depths of your passion. These men will be full of feeling and capable of taking responsibility for an intimate relationship if other things are right in their planetary patterns.

MERCURY

The Desire to Think

Mercury is a planet which shows us how we think and how we communicate. It tries to communicate what the ego needs to say, write, or express. Since Mercury is very close to the Sun, the desire to survive, it is closely connected to the ego. Mercury seeks to organize information and help fulfill the ego's purpose. The Greek god Mercury was the "messenger of the gods." It seeks to connect the desires of the other planets and translates their feelings and impulses across to others. Mercury is the planet of speech, thought, and logic. It connects one part of our psyche with another through these processes. Its primary function is to make sense out of what it receives from the planetary energies connected to it. Like the Moon, Mercury is greatly "colored" by the solar field it is in at birth and by any planet related to it. The larger planets seem to have protocol or dominance over these smaller planets. Favorable energies from other planets enhance the communication skills between people. Unfavorable energies obstruct them.

MERCURY IN THE 12 SOLAR FIELDS

Mercury In The Aries Solar Field - Fire
KEY PHRASE:
> *"I think fast. My mind is on fire. I sometimes wear myself out with so many ideas firing away in my brain."*

As you can see from the description on page 50, the fire of the Aries field can excite the mind. The person with this placement could have a mind that runs like a motor with the switch always on. The mind works fast and constantly — always thinking, always thinking, until it tumbles into exhaustion. A person with this position may have headaches because their mind is often on fire and their brain can get overheated. They need to keep a cool head and a calm mind. They can be blunt and inconsiderate in their speech because they are so quick to react they do not take time to consider the consequences. This is a mind of great enthusiasm and has the potential to be very creative, but the fire needs to be harnessed. They usually communicate well with people who have fire and air energies in their nature. (Gemini, Leo, Libra, Sagittarius, and Aquarius.)

Mercury In The Taurus Solar Field - Earth
KEY PHRASE:
> *"I think slowly because I need time to work out my projects. Don't push me for a decision. I will only resist you."*

Here Mercury is colored by the earth attitude of Taurus. The mind is in a field that is just the opposite of Aries. The mental energies here are very slow, methodical, and predictable. A person with this placement needs to have a lot of freedom to do their own work in their own time. They cannot be pushed to "get the report out." They will get it done, but they need a lot of time on their own. These people tend to be good researchers, because they do not miss details, and they are excellent builders. They love form and structure and may spend hours going over an idea persistently until it bears fruit. They are very tenacious mentally and communicate well with earth and water energies. (Cancer, Virgo, Scorpio, Capricorn, and Pisces.)

Mercury In The Gemini Solar Field - Air
KEY PHRASE:
> "I think extremely fast and can handle two things at once. It is hard for me to finish projects because I get bored so easily."

Here, Mercury truly lives in the head. This person is very mental, quick-witted, silver-tongued, and clever as a crow in this solar field. This is the realm of air and they live in the lofty realm of ideas and sometimes in the depth of clever evasion from the truth. They can be double-minded, double-tongued (or forked tongue, as the Indians used to say), and a weaver of tales. They will tell little lies of convenience to get out of a fix. They are always seeking harmony but have so much interest in so many things that they have a hard time living up to promises to themselves as well as to others. They can come forth with the most clever and bright ideas but may have a difficult time using them because they get bored too easily and therefore fail to capitalize on them Their greatest lesson is to learn to finish the projects they start. They communicate very well with the air and fire energies of Aries, Leo, Libra, Sagittarius, and Aquarius.

Mercury In The Cancer Solar Field - Water
KEY PHRASE
> "I think with my feelings. Therefore, my thoughts are colored with my emotions. Objectivity is hard for me. I concentrate on security."

Here the mind falls into water, which is the realm of feeling and mood changes. The thought process are more psychic or intuitive than logical. These people feel with their mind. Their thinking is centered on home, family, and security. They can be good at selling any products that have to with the home, family, or real estate because they naturally understand the needs of home buyers. They have given a great deal of thought to these areas so are well qualified to persuade others to their choice. They may have interests in architecture, carpentry, landscaping, baking, or owning a restaurant where they can sell food. Since their mind is centered on the home, they know how to plan good meals, feed everyone well, and make them feel comfortable and secure. They like the whole idea of mothering, nurturing, and being nurtured. They can express some crabby or picky attitudes at times because of the changing moods of their thought processes. They usually communicate well with the water and earth energies (Scorpio, Pisces, Taurus, Virgo, and Capricorn.)

Mercury In The Leo Solar Field - Fire

Key Phrase:

"I think proudly, creatively, and artistically, and like to be honored for my ideas. I have a stubborn mind because I don't like to change my opinions."

Leo imparts the attitude of importance and being right. The mental attitude is usually one of superiority and basic dominance. There is a great deal of mental pride: where the person often describes his or her achievements as if the world revolved around them. This could be described as mental arrogance. But behind this arrogance is a basic insecurity. If this person does not get to keep the center stage, you may find them sulking or not participating in any joint effort. They feel their ideas are of great importance and are very tenacious in clinging to them. However, they can speak with great eloquence and be very persuasive because of the energy that radiates from their speech. Their voice can persuade the listener to great emotion.

They may be very good at theatrical performances, art, music, radio, or television. They think about love affairs and emotional expressions of the heart, but the attention and thrill of an affair could be more important than being centered on real love. They can appear to be very romantic, speaking words like fine silk, but depth of intimacy may be lacking. They usually communicate well with Aquarius, Gemini, Sagittarius, Aries, and Libra.

Mercury In The Virgo Solar Field - Earth
KEY PHRASE
> *"I think in detail. I am thoughtful, particular, efficient, and know how to organize my life. I can't stand disorder. I like to do things right."*

Mercury is very much at home in this earthy field because it is strongly influenced by the tendency to think critically. The mind is usually absorbed in detailing, organizing, discarding, weighing, and analyzing in the pursuit of the perfect method. Of course the perfect method is never reached but the process goes on anyway. Where others may make foolish and poorly timed decisions, this person has already thought everything through. They seem to have a sixth sense of how to function best in any practical endeavor. Therefore, they can be excellent at law, chemistry, medicine, or other fields that require detailed analysis of materials. They lose sight of the bigger picture and can be critical to a fault. They will generally fuss over every little paper clip in the office or become very upset if something is out of place. They usually like to help other people solve problems because they have a deep need to be of service, and if approached from this position, they will be the first to volunteer. They are usually very dependable and will "get the job done." They communicate well with Capricorn, Taurus, Scorpio, Pisces, and Cancer.

Mercury In The Libra Solar Field - Air
KEY PHRASE:
> "I think in terms of harmony, cooperation and sharing. I like to express artistic ideas. I often have trouble with indecision."

The energy of Libra is expressed in working with opposites. Mercury here finds itself expressing beautiful words, beautiful sounds, and seeking harmonious relationships. Songs may be made and sung with great emotion. Peace and harmony between two opposing parties may be achieved through the convincing words of a Mercury in Libra, or a great romantic novel may touch the hearts of dreamers everywhere. They may be effective marriage counselors because of an ability to see both sides. They are intensely interested in the group and its joint achievement, therefore they can be effective at public relations or handling large gatherings. Although there is a need to find harmony with everyone and everything, the search is not always successful because a basic idealism or pretense may not match reality. They can also play both ends against the middle and be accused of being two-faced. Some types can be tormented by having to make decisions, because they may have to take a stand for one side over another. A very difficult position for Libra to accept. The energy fields of Gemini, Aquarius, Leo, Sagittarius, and Aries are most harmonious with them.

Mercury In the Scorpio Solar Field - Water
KEY PHRASE:
> "I think deeply, secretively, and like to be in control of my own ideas. I like to work out my plans in solitude and make independent decisions."

You may think that this person should be very flexible with their Mercury in a water field, because water is pliable and adaptable to its environment. But this water field is frozen. It is ice. Therefore the mind is fixed and tenacious in its opinions and it is almost impossible to change once the individual has accepted an idea to be true. To be wrong is something this person would almost never admit, because true humility is difficult. There seems to be a deep abiding pride in whatever ideas this person holds on to, almost as if those ideas were sacred and etched in stone. This is a shrewd, deep, and penetrating mind that knows how to solve problems. The person with this Mercury can be a good detective, resolve difficult situations and find the answers to subtle mysteries. Few things in human nature escape their attention, for they see from a deeper level. They may be silent in the expression of their opinions, appearing to know nothing. But one day they will cut through your own defenses and find a feeling in you that you never knew you possessed. Never blame them or accuse them of anything and you will have their abiding loyalty. In general, they communicate well with Pisces, Taurus, Capricorn, Cancer, and Virgo.

Mercury In The Sagittarius Solar Field - Fire
KEY PHRASE:
> "I think deeply and seek to understand the meaning of life. I will often skip the details to get the bigger picture."

Here the mind is full of the fire of adventure, always reaching out across the horizon to another place. This mind may utter prophetic truths or talk endlessly about the daily adventures of life. It is an expansive mind that is interested in principles and has no patience for details. It is only interested in the larger picture. The ultimate meaning. The mind may be focused on law because of some deep need to find justice for others or to enjoy the game. This is a forthright mind not in search of subtlety. It holds on strongly to truth. This is a fair and honest mind and could rarely be deceptive. However there is sometimes an unkind streak in the words they speak, perhaps not by intent, but by sheer and brutal honesty about the way they see things. You may not like what they say, but you are never in doubt as to where they stand. At times, they seem totally fearless, and will stand up to anyone. They could be engaged in publishing, writing, teaching, and philosophy. They have favorable communications with Aries, Leo, Gemini, Aquarius, and Libra.

Mercury In The Capricorn Solar Field - Earth
KEY PHRASE:
> "I think in practical terms, what can be explained. I'm only interested in the task at hand and the bottom line."

The realm of Capricorn is a place of the sensible, practical, and useful. A Mercury here is primarily interested in the facts, what is provable by science and practical experience. The mind functions in the realm of practical materialism. This is a very serious mind with a basic understanding of its own gravity. This person seeks to find humor in things. They know they need to "lighten up" but they are conditioned to think seriously. Humor is their best medicine. They usually are good thinkers in business matters because they are very realistic and only interested in the bottom line. What are the true results? If it doesn't work, throw it away, or use it for something else. They need to cultivate some mysticism because they tend to get locked into the factual or material considerations of daily existence. They usually adhere to tradition and what went before them and are strong believers in the motto "if it ain't broke, don't fix it." They communicate well with Taurus, Virgo, Cancer, Scorpio, and Pisces.

Mercury In The Aquarius Solar Field - Air
KEY PHRASE:
> "I think about the unusual and unpredictable because I have a desire to explore the edge of experience. I like to solve unique problems and go my own way. Some people think I am mentally arrogant."

Here is a very independent mind, usually full of original insights. They always seek the different, the unusual, and the creative. This is usually a very bright mind full of awareness and unique ideas. They look beyond the obvious and can present a perspective no one else ever conceived. They can be very musical and express a world of harmonies no one has ever heard before. A search through the lives of the greatest creators would no doubt show us that many of them had Mercury in Aquarius. Although usually very smart, Aquarian Mercury people tend to express their awareness arrogantly. At times, their speech can be so blunt, impersonal, and unfeeling, that they cause others to avoid them. Because of this, they often fail to illicit cooperation from their friends. This can be very disappointing to them because their friends are very important to them. However, they do not hang around licking any wounds. They are usually off to the next adventure because they have a great capacity for mental detachment. Aries, Gemini, Leo, Libra, and Sagittarius can usually communicate well with them.

Mercury In The Pisces Solar Field - Water
KEY PHRASE:
> "I do not think logically. I think with my feelings and am very psychic. My mind often wanders off into fantasy and imagination. Sometimes I can read other people's thoughts."

Here the mind is lost in an ocean of feeling. This is not a logical or thinking mind. It is very psychic and intuitive. The person with this Mercury needs to reach their conclusions on a reliable hunch. This mind can soar and travel to the depths of art, imagination, or clairvoyance. A person with this Mercury senses and feels the subtle influences around them. They are very attuned to these psychic subtleties, often reading people's thoughts and feelings. They will sometimes say, "He is going to call me" and the phone will ring with that person on the other end. The person with this Mercury needs to protect herself from negative influences, or people who think negatively, because they will absorb those thoughts and think that they are their own. They should surround themselves with positive and beautiful surroundings so that they are free to sense their own inner world without outside influences. They seem to communicate best with Cancer, Scorpio, Taurus, Capricorn, and Virgo.

9

The Five Transpersonal Planets and Their Effects

The positive effect of a transpersonal planet occurs when it is related to a personal planet by sextile (60 degrees) or trine (120 degrees) and sometimes by conjunction (0 degrees). The negative effect of a transpersonal planet occurs when it is related to a personal planet by square and sometimes by conjunction. This "sometimes by conjunction" will be explained as we continue. (Review Chapter 7, "The Four Major Planetary Effects".)

It is important to understand that the planets are part of you. They are not separate from you; they are you! If you see another person's planet hitting your Mars, this means that something inside of you is being affected. It is not just hitting your Mars. It is hitting a part of you. It is affecting a chakra. A subtle nerve center within you. It is affecting you. Always keep this in mind. If a man's planet hits your Mars, he stirs a desire or reaction in you in some way. Once you find out what planet makes contact with your Mars, check within yourself first to see how he stirs your feelings. Then confirm these feelings with the information you find in the following pages. For example, if his Uranus is sitting on your Venus (conjunct) ask yourself what you feel in his company. (For me, it was sex at first sight. See page 38.) If a woman or man have their Saturn on your Mars, you will probably hate being around them because they inhibit and frustrate you. It is always best to describe your feelings first to yourself before you find out what planet is involved. Then confirm this feeling by reading that section in this book which explains the effect another person's planet has upon a planet in your birthchart. If a man's Saturn is conjunct your Mars, see pages 147-148. A conjunction of Saturn on Mars is usually very negative. If a man's Venus is conjunct your Mars or vise versa, you have a strong sexual attraction. See the basic effects of Venus with Mars on page 171.

JUPITER

Desire to Acquire

While Jupiter is a very large planet, it does not seem to bring great experiences as a visiting planet. Although Jupiter shows the desire within us to expand our horizons, to believe and hope for better things, the things he promises are often just full of hot air. But he can bring an opportunity for you to acquire that which you seek. He is a pleasant planet, but prone to excess, exaggeration, and pretense. He brings the feeling that everything is possible, full of hope, and therefore he is the planet of great support and optimism. He has dominion over law, publishing, religion, foreign countries, long journeys, higher education, and distant travels. He is expansive by nature. The best way to look at the effects of Jupiter when it makes contact with a personal planet is to expect some kind of increase. Keep in mind that he often promises but seldom delivers. So don't expect too much from this fellow when he is a visitor. However, he can be very supportive if favorably connected in relationships.

THE FIVE TRANSPERSONAL PLANETS AND THEIR EFFECTS

Jupiter's positive effects on the Sun: This contact by conjunction, sextile, or trine is very positive. If Jupiter is in any of these relationships to your Sun at birth, you are a very positive person. You bring hope and an abundance of energy to those around you. Here Jupiter expands and seems to scatter the Sun's energies in all directions and, therefore, has a warming effect on all that he touches. Obviously, if someone brings his Jupiter to your Sun, he brings you hope, support, opportunity, and possibility. This is a very positive connection.

Jupiter's negative effects on the Sun: If Jupiter's contact is by square at birth, this person has to be aware of exaggerating his position in life. The ego can feel too important and excesses can drain energy and health.

If someone brings you this kind of Jupiter, beware of them promising more than they can deliver or leading you into wasting your own resources on their pipe dreams. They could also lead you into the physical excesses of food and drink.

Jupiter's positive effects on the Moon: When positive contacts are formed, Jupiter is a great support to the emotions. This person is a great sustainer of other people — always there to help them — and they feel it. They are also very resourceful in finding creative ways to sustain themselves financially and have an uncanny ability to find opportunities where others fail.

If someone brings their Jupiter to your Moon in a positive way (conjunction, sextile, or trine), you will always feel nurtured and sustained by them. They will try to give you anything you need. You are blessed by their company.

Jupiter's negative effects on the Moon: If Jupiter's contact is negative (square) in relation to the Moon, the situation is very different. The need to support their own place in the world takes precedence over others and there is a lack of sympathy with their needs. They may promise help, but others will find their offer less than real.

The negative impact of another person's Jupiter on your Moon is to lead you into excess or promise you more than they can ever deliver. Look for the results before investing too much energy in their suggestions. They could lead you to believe things that are simply not true.

Jupiter's positive effects on Venus: The positive contact of Jupiter to Venus is very beneficial. A person born with this planetary pattern, is considered very fortunate. Since Venus rules money, love, and relationship, all these areas of life can be full of happy experiences. It is said that this person tends to be at the right place at the right time. Even if they were to back away from success, they would back into it. They probably have good friends, love people, and are very social. Anyone who brings his Jupiter to your Venus in a positive way, can be the channel of wealth for you. He will support your needs and desires completely and even try to get you anything you want.

Jupiter's negative effects on Venus: When someone else's Jupiter forms an adverse relationship to another person's Venus, they can be led into excesses and waste their resources. These are the fair weather friends who are never around when we need them.

An unfavorable Venus/Jupiter pattern (the square), leads the individual to seek a life of excess in money, food, and sex. They could lose money through unsafe speculation because they exaggerate their expectations. They find it hard to become truly intimate with others for fear of the demands that might be made upon them. This pattern makes Venus a selfish goddess — she will not go out of her way for others, because she is too busy fulfilling her own excessive desires.

Jupiter's positive effects on Mars: Here Jupiter adds a great increase of energy. Since Mars is already an aggressive planet, a positive impact from Jupiter can give tremendous energy. If Mars is favorably connected to Jupiter from birth, this person may be so full of energy they rarely rest. This contact also increases the sexual drive and there is a tendency to overdo everything. Their sexual aura can be overwhelming for some people. But if you are looking for sheer energy, you can't beat this pattern. Many great and wonderful enterprises can be completed because of so much available energy. Even though this is an impulsive energy, if it is controlled, it can serve us well. If someone brings a positive contact to your Mars (conjunction, sextile, or trine) they will support your ambitions and add their energy to help you achieve whatever goal you want. They will fill you with enthusiasm and creative ideas and show you how it is possible to fulfill your own plans.

Jupiter's negative effects on Mars: If a person has this pattern from birth, they are basically rash in their actions, bite off more than they can chew, and find it hard to plan and stay organized. Their enthusiasm often gets the best of them and they will have to do things over again because they do not have the patience to work out the details before acting.

If another person's Jupiter makes a negative contact with your Mars, then they can persuade you to act rashly or prematurely. Together, you become much more impulsive and find a certain impatience frustrating your lives. This contact will never be boring but it could be exhausting and lead to many premature decisions.

Jupiter's positive effects on Mercury: Jupiter adds zest to the mind in this position. The mind has a thirst for knowledge and keen curiosity. The mind seeks to communicate on a grand scale. Some of our greatest writers had this planetary partnership. There is usually an excellent memory and a great storehouse of knowledge immediately accessible. The accent is on communication. This is an excellent gift for journalists, speakers, philosophers, linguists, planners, writers, and people who do a lot of thinking.

If another person's Jupiter relates favorably to your Mercury, they will help you in your communications and add many helpful ideas for any project you might engage. They support your thinking and give you confidence in your mental pursuits. You may find yourself talking a lot in their company. This is because they stimulate your thinking.

Jupiter's negative effects on Mercury: In this situation, the individual with this position in their own patterns, are prone to exaggeration and overstepping their ability to get things done. They take on more than they can handle because there is a strong, outreaching tendency that causes them to bite off projects in big hunks. Then they cannot digest them. There is usually a serious need for organization and planning. Otherwise, little gets done. They love starting things but show little patience for finishing them. Their mind is always racing but they do not know where to go with their ideas.

The negative effect of another person's Jupiter can lead you into undertaking enterprises that have great promise but little substance in reality. The Jupiter enthusiasm may affect your judgment and cause you to make rash decisions. It is best to check all promises thoroughly before investing time and money. You will soon learn to take what this person promises or says with great restraint. This is simply their effect upon you. It will not necessarily be true in their relationship to another person. They are simply motivated to add enthusiasm to your thinking but may cause you to make wrong judgments in your decisions.

SATURN

Desire to Separate

This is a planet you always want to take seriously, because his impact has a serious effect. Saturn is the desire within us to separate from others, to protect ourselves

THE FIVE TRANSPERSONAL PLANETS AND THEIR EFFECTS

from being hurt, and to defend ourselves against a hostile world. Saturn works against intimacy, therefore the feelings he arouses have to be confronted and understood because they are basically feelings of fear that work against intimacy.

Regardless of our great fantasies and dreams, Saturn is about reality. It is the reality of this world — not the next one. It deals only with "the bottom line," the results, and the material world. He rules the world of business where only results count. His cold and serious nature does not support the five personal planets. He rules the energy field of Capricorn, the "dead of winter," and Saturn's negative contact with the personal planets usually brings some kind of denial, fear, or loss. Only a sextile (60 degrees apart) or trine (120 degrees apart) contact will support the other planets involved. There seems to be some kind of unfinished business involved when Saturn is in the picture. He is always the teacher, but usually the lessons are hard to learn. Although I like the character-building power of Saturn, I can't give him much praise when it comes to supporting relationships.

Saturn's positive effects on the Sun: These are the sextile and trine positions only — not the conjunction. Saturn always has a stabilizing influence when related positively to another planet. When related this way to the Sun from birth, it enables this person to discipline their energies so they can accomplish the goals of survival (Sun). It helps bring out positive results of the energy field in which the Sun is found at birth. For instance, if your Sun is in Capricorn, Saturn's positive relationship would enable you to bring out all the better qualities of the Capricorn nature, e.g., business ability, organizational skills, and leadership.

Obviously, if someone else's Saturn is related to your Sun in a positive way, they would help you achieve your goals by lending ideas and suggestions for supporting your ambitions. This is a very fruitful connection that can bring many positive results.

Saturn's negative effects on the Sun: Here the conjunction and square adversely affect the Sun. Since the Sun expresses the desire to survive (the ego), negative effects of Saturn can really hinder the ego's freedom of expression. There is usually a lack of confidence, self-doubt, and fear of pushing forward. This situation can be traced to this person's relationship to their father, mother, or to the principal authority in their childhood. This is a conditioning of doubt of self and the will to get what they want. This person may have to work very hard to get what they need, and when they do, they will earn it. They do not feel like anything is going to be easy and expect to work hard for everything they get. So, they usually do just that.

If someone else's Saturn is afflicting your Sun, you will not want to associate with them. You will feel inhibited, obstructed, and unsupported. They will tend to criticize you. These are not favorable patterns for business, marriage, or working together to achieve mutual goals. It is best not to have to work or even associate with this person. If you do, you could be headed for misery. They will always find the worst in you.

Saturn's positive effects on the Moon: As we have seen, the Moon is our sense of being sustained or nurtured by life. Saturn's positive effect (the sextile and trine) on the Moon at birth shows that this person feels emotionally sustained by life. An authority figure in their youth (father or mother or whoever was in charge of their childhood) had a positive influence on their habits. The discipline they received as a child was tempered with good will and genuine caring for their welfare. Probably a firm, but gentle hand guided them in such a way that they feel supported emotionally by their own good sense of self and judgment. This planetary pattern supported them emotionally as they were growing up so they have an inherent feeling of self-reliance.

Of course, anyone whose Saturn relates to your Moon in this way will also be very helpful and support your needs for security and well-being. You will be able to rely upon them.

Saturn's negative effects on the Moon: A person born with Saturn conjunct or square their Moon, will need to practice "staying in the sunlight" because Saturn here darkens the Moon's spirit. This means that the childhood was austere and without real emotional warmth from the family — especially the mother. It is important to understand that this environment may have conditioned them to feel sorrowful — that they did not get the nurturing and support that every child needs. As an adult, they may have occasional bouts with depressions and experience heavy moods because their feelings wander back to these unhappy scenes. At some point, they may want to change these unconscious memories through guided hypnotherapy.

Obviously, if someone else brings a negative Saturn to your Moon, they will depress you and you will not want to be around them. It is also important to see if your own Saturn affects your child, your mate, or some other person who is close to you in this way. It will explain why they react to you the way they do. You can have compassion for them. It is usually not something that you would consciously be doing but the other person may read that repressive and critical feelings are coming from you on a subtle level. It will take some observation to understand the specific reasons for their reactions.

Saturn's positive effects on Venus: Only the sextile and the trine have positive effects on Venus. Venus is a very human planet that shows what we value, like, appreciate, and prefer. It rules money and relationships. Therefore when it is related positively to Saturn, Venus feels sustained and supported by the material world. Saturn imparts feelings of loyalty in affection to friends and lovers and honors business transactions. If these planetary patterns are present at the time of birth, this person has the endearing qualities of steadfastness, reliability, and honesty in her relationships. They are usually good at handling money and have a cautious attitude about spending on frivolous things. In matters of love, they are the "true blue" type and take relationships quite seriously.

If another person's Saturn relates favorable to your Venus, you will feel that they support your sense of self worth and will also be there for you when you need their help. This would be a good relationship for working together in business because it generates a sincere cooperation that makes success possible.

Saturn's negative effects on Venus: The effect of a conjunction or square can be quite difficult, because Saturn robs us of the sense of self-worth, worldly benefits, and leads us into abusive relationships. If these patterns exist at birth, the lifelong journey will be in trying to prove that we are good, that we don't deserve to be abused, and that we need nurturing and support like everyone else. We may tend to sacrifice in life, become the victim, because we were criticized as a child and did not feel loved or supported. We tend to attract those people who do not love us and engage in relationships where we have to do all the giving and make all the concessions just to get a little attention from our mate. They usually are not worth all our giving, but we may not be used to getting what we want, so we tend to endure these insults. This conditioning can be overcome through creative hypnotherapy and by pursuing that which we love. We must not be so willing to be the sacrifice. We must go after what is good for us and reject those who do not support us. This will hurt, but we will soon realize self-love if we do this. We will refuse to be someone else's lover if we don't love them. Sooner or later we will discover that we are a very valuable person and deserve to have the best like anyone else.

If someone brings a negative Saturn to you (conjunct or square your Venus), turn around and walk off in the opposite direction. They will not give you what you want. If you have to establish a relationship with them, you will find that you are the one who is expected to be the giver. You cannot possibly come out ahead. The problem is that you may feel guilty or obligated to them. But don't give into these feelings. This is a trap. Avoid it at all costs. It is important to remember that this person is not necessarily bad. They are simply bad for you.

Saturn's positive effects on Mars: Only the sextile or trine are positive here. Think of Mars as an energy that makes things happen. It is naturally aggressive because it supports the survival instinct in all of us. We all have to go after things to survive. But this energy can be expressed aggressively, creatively, wildly, or with hostility. It depends on how Mars is affected by the other planets. A positive influence from Saturn enables Mars to work efficiently without any waste of energy. If this is the way your Mars is related to Saturn, then you have the ability to get things done without wasting your time on wrong starts or impulsive behavior. There is a certain positive restraint in everything you do. You know how to complete your projects in the shortest available time. You have the ability to focus your energy and concentrate on the task at hand without getting distracted.

If another person brings you a favorable Saturn, they will help you complete projects and show you a better way to do things. This is a positive support for joint enterprises and for achieving goals together. The sextile and trine relationship of Saturn to your Mars is always harmonious because the elements work in harmony.

Saturn's negative effects on Mars: Here the energies of Mars are repressed by the conjunction or square. This person has to be careful with this energy because there is potential violence due to an inner rage. There is usually some kind of anger associated with a repressed Mars. Saturn is the repressor. This person needs to find positive release for his energy and be careful in his association with people. Somewhere in his childhood someone "sat on him" and he is resentful for that. Therefore, anyone in his adult world who tries to sit on him should be very careful. There could be a fight.

If someone brings you a negative Saturn, you will feel very repressed by them. They represent a real obstruction to your intentions. It is best to find a way out of this relationship as it will eventually create problems. If that is not possible, then you will have to bite the bullet or seek a compromise. Also, should you have your Saturn related negatively to another person, you might be repressing or controlling them without realizing it. It is wise to check out your planetary patterns with them if you suspect something is wrong.

Saturn's positive effects on Mercury: Actually, Saturn is not much of a friend to many planets. Even though he may be related to Mercury in a positive way, he still adds a serious quality to the mind. Here the mind is able to carry out the expression of its ideas efficiently and to express them fully through discipline. It shows that the mind could be too serious, prone to depression and self doubt, even though it is capable of deep and serious thought. This person can think and write for long hours without a rest because they have a disciplined mind. This is a positive pattern for scientific work involving research and can give power to the thoughts so that they can create form and meaning out of chaos.

If someone brings Saturn to your Mercury in a favorable way (sextile, trine, and sometimes conjunction), they can add practical advice and depth to your understanding and help clarify your thinking for you. This connection could add a new dimension to your relationship and make you feel supported by the other person's practical suggestions.

This could be a good pattern for business pursuits and produce solid results.

Saturn's negative effects on Mercury: These positions affect the mind in a negative way. These people do not trust their mind, hate studying, and have inherited painful memories relating to school and learning experiences. They may feel blocked in saying what they think, or simply unclear about what they do think. They could have a fear of speaking before large groups of people. Their tongues sometimes gets tied. Stuttering is possible. They are capable of deep thought but doubt their mental abilities. They may stick to the tried and true ways of thinking without venturing into creative realms. They do not want to take risks. This connection could limit their thinking. The limitations may not really be there, but they are set up to believe they are. These basic inhibitions may relate back to the first teacher or a critical parent's remark when they were studying at an early age.

If another person's Saturn relates to your Mercury in a negative way, they can be your worst critic. They don't think your ideas are worth much and will not support the projects you create. They always seem to find something wrong with what you say, write, or express in meetings. Basically, there is just a lack of support for any of your communications. It is rare that their criticism would be constructive for you.

URANUS

Desire for Independence

This is a very radical and volatile planet that will not tolerate any form of restriction. Uranus represents the desire within us to be different, to be independent and not follow the herd. It seeks to find its own unique way in the world. It is that part within us that hates to take orders, bend to authority, or follow other people's advice.

Uranus has a sudden, unpredictable quality. It often brings the unexpected. "I just turned the corner and there he was" or "it hit me from out of no where" are statements people tend to make when Uranus is involved. Uranus is also a very creative planet because contacts with it tend to push us in new directions. It can add brilliance, uniqueness of action and unusual artistic expressions. Consider four Aquarian spirits who were ruled by the planet Uranus and you will get the idea: Mozart, Schubert, Edison, and Jerome Kern. All of these very unique individuals expressed great originality in their work. Uranus can also add a cruel side to the nature. It seems indifferent to personal feelings and holds a certain detachment from others. People with positive connections to Uranus are special individuals. If the connections are negative, they can be downright obnoxious.

Uranus' positive effects on the Sun: This energy gives the Sun a strong impulse to explore the unusual. The ego is in search of new ways to express itself. This energy is very creative, full of life and originality. If you have this placement at birth, you look for and are attracted to men who are offbeat and unusual. You are strongly attracted to a man who is quite different from the normal herd. When you "fall in love" it is usually at first sight, but you can be bored just as quickly. What you really have to offer to the world is a unique perspective of life and an individuality that inspires others to be adventurous. You may have difficulty staying with one man due to an overt desire for new adventures. This is because you are something of a character yourself. You are considered "different" by others.

If another person brings this Uranus to your Sun, they could inspire you to try new experiences and lead you into radical encounters with life.

Uranus' negative effects on the Sun: If Uranus makes this contact with the Sun, this person will have the desire to break away from established conditions. They set their own conditions. They are strongly independent and are unlikely to cooperate with others. Their ego may be so strong that they have very little tolerance for rules, regulations, authority and routine. Cooperation and compromise are important virtues for them to learn, but they will have to do that on their own terms.

If someone brings you a negative Uranus to your Sun, they will bring a wild and unpredictable energy into your life. They will "push your buttons," lead you to take foolish chances and challenge your will. The ego is very strong and uncooperative. This is a very unreliable person who can be here today and gone tomorrow. They can steal your heart and never give it back. Don't invest a lot of energy and expectation in them. If you do, you will set yourself up for disappointment.

Uranus' positive effects on the Moon: A person born with this position, has habits that are most unusual. They do not hold on to experiences very long and therefore are not sentimental and rarely look back to lick their wounds. They have an impatience for solving problems and are quick to get to the heart of a solution. They can be very impulsive. However, they are very interesting people full of new and unusual ideas and most of us like to be around them. Life is never boring when they are around.

If someone brings a positive Uranus to your Moon they can be responsible for getting you out of a rut. They will upset your normal surroundings, your expectations, and urge you to change your habits. This can be a very positive influence. They can show you many possibilities to your own life goals.

Uranus' negative effects on the Moon: This person could have a hair-trigger temper and surprise us with their reactions. They can explode when they are pressured to do something they don't want to do. They do not take kindly to any form of domination from others, and you will certainly hear from them if you attempt to tell them what to do. They are fiercely independent, but people may avoid them because of their volatile temperament. Since the Moon is involved, this anger could relate to reactions to the mother or to women. Violence could result.

If someone brings you a negative Uranus, then they can upset you more than any other person. They can stir reactions within you that you never thought you had. They can "get your goat." They can also make you feel very nervous and cause you to feel constantly agitated in their company.

Uranus' positive effects on Venus: Since Venus is the desire to seek beauty, love, and relationship, the planet Uranus here adds to the uniqueness of this search. Anyone born with this position, seeks fulfillment in unique ways. They can express themselves with great originality in music, art, design, or style. They are always open to new relationships. They love to be with creative people who can stimulate their insatiable desire for new and exciting encounters. Because they like to associate with the unusual, they learn a lot of things other people don't even know about. They could be lucky with money and posses a sixth sense of how to invest it. There can be sudden financial gain. Their life is never boring because they cannot stand boredom. They live on the edge of relationships because they believe in the freedom of love and the adventure of new encounters.

If someone brings their Uranus to your Venus in a positive way, they will urge you to explore places you have never seen. They can stimulate you to a sudden love experience. They can cause you to fall quickly in love, but the attraction may not last because the need for constant stimulation creates a strain on the relationship. Sooner or later, one of you will not be able to keep up the pace. This person can inspire you to create something unique and lasting if you are an artist. They will help you see through different eyes.

Uranus' negative effects on Venus: A person born with this kind of pattern, can be very inconstant and unreliable in their feelings. They seem to feel that if they commit to one person, they will lose the opportunity to be with another. But behind this strategy lies the real truth. They don't want to be vulnerable. They seem to feel that if someone has their heart, that would destroy their freedom. So they always tend to dance around the idea of intimacy but rarely truly engage it. Their need to seek out another relationship even while they are with someone is simply an avoidance of true intimacy. In true intimacy, we give our heart away. This person is afraid to do that.

If someone else's Uranus relates to your Venus in a negative way, they may seduce you into an affair because they stimulate your sexual energies by spinning your chakras. But be aware. The relationship may not last long. This kind of contact tends to be short-lived. This person can also lead you into financial excess and cause you to waste your resources through wild enterprises. Think carefully before getting involved with them.

Uranus' positive effects on Mars: If Uranus is related in a positive way to a person's Mars, it creates an unusual character full of the spirit of adventure. They like to explore unknown territory and do things no one else has ever done before. They will take up a challenge even when they know it is risky just to prove their uniqueness. They like being first at everything. They are willing to take risks where others hesitate. They are competitive and have the will and courage to win at large enterprises. They are not afraid to take a chance. They may be outstanding in sports that require great skill and physical strength.

If someone brings a positive Uranus to your Mars, they can inspire you to act with courage and give you the confidence you may need to take action. They offer you a new way of doing things and can help get you out of a rut. You will find them very interesting and fascinating. Since

Mars is also a sexual planet, this can mean love or sex at first sight. This contact can be very stimulating and you will need to be aware of the tendency to excess. You could become exhausted through mere association with them.

Uranus' negative effects on Mars: The negative effect of Uranus (square) promotes a wild and sometimes foolish lifestyle. This person will need to practice caution in all of their undertakings because they are always pushing their boundaries beyond what most of us call good sense. Like the positive Uranus, they also take unnecessary risks just to prove a point, but they usually lose in the doing and may suffer a serious accident or cause something regrettable to happen. They should be careful with any kind of machinery as they tend to overlook safety precautions. When they push their boundaries and try to do things no one else has ever done, they may end up flat on their face. This is definitely the kind of planetary pattern which says, "Don't push your luck."

If someone else has his Uranus in a negative relationship to your Mars, he will prompt you to act against good judgment and lead you into experiences that could be risky for you. Always think twice before doing anything he suggests. If there is a sexual connection between you, don't expect the relationship to last or turn out the way you want it. There is always something unpredictable in this kind of relationship. Take care.

Uranus' positive effects on Mercury: A person born with this pattern is very bright. They are advanced in their understanding and have a very sharp mind. The conjunction is the most positive because the thinking processes are filled with original ideas. This is a mind that knows that it knows and is capable of achieving a high position in life if so desired.

If another person brings Uranus to your Mercury in a positive way, they add clarity and brilliance to your own thinking and you are greatly inspired by their presence.

You see them as a source of knowledge and you like the mental stimulation they bring to you. You could work extremely well together and bring forth some very unusual ideas that would benefit you both. They would enjoy your interest in them and you would be inspired by their unique insights.

Uranus' negative effects on Mercury: This could be a pattern of agitated impatience. The mind is bright but has a streak of intolerance for slower thinkers. There is a certain amount of arrogance and pride of knowledge. This could be the person who "knows it all." They do get flashes of insight that startle people but their obnoxious way of showing it may be a "turn off". They are impatient and intolerant of other people's ideas and appear to be very insensitive to another person's viewpoint.

Anyone who's Uranus affects your Mercury in an adverse way, will challenge your thinking. They will not simply criticize your mind but they will steamroll over it. They may oppose your ideas and interrupt you when you are speaking or simply refuse to associate with you. They will find what they call "holes in your thinking". It may even be humorous to them, but they are obnoxious to you.

NEPTUNE

Desire for Ecstasy

Neptune is a most mysterious planet because its energy works on a subtle level. It gives us the urge for ecstasy, to seek peak experiences, and to transcend the trials and troubles of the world through romantic love, art, beauty, film, music, writing, poetry, or self-transcendence. These are its positive expressions. A strong Neptune can give us the need to get away from the world; to escape it through positive or negative channels according to how it affects our other planetary patterns. On the negative side, this desire for ecstasy can move people toward drugs, alcohol, fantasy, deception, weakness, dependency, swindling, lying, cheating, and stealing. (Is there a street drug called "ecstasy"?)

This is an important planet for determining ancient connections that you may have with some of the people you contact here. You will discover if such connections exist in your relationships by exploring the kind of contact other people's Neptune makes with your own planetary patterns. If you find these connections, you will understand why the feelings you hold for such people are so extraordinary.

Neptune's positive effects on the Sun: Neptune manifests in the realm of the unseen. Therefore, its effects are subtle. Since its expression within us is the desire for ecstasy, its contact with our personal planets arouses this impulse. If Neptune relates to a person's Sun at birth in a positive way by sextile or trine, it can impart the highest aspirations. They are very interested in the subtle things of life and they consider love to be beyond this world. They are very sensitive to other people's needs and cannot endure the suffering of another person without wanting to do something to help them. They have to be careful about creating illusions about their friends and lovers. They are sometimes too open and trusting because they see good qualities in just about everyone. They can be very musical, artistic, and creative with deep imagination. Since the Sun is masculine, the father could have been an alcoholic or not there emotionally to support this person. The conjunction is sometimes positive and sometimes negative. It depends how we respond to life. If you are well-grounded, you can handle your flights of imagination and need to help others, but you must still be careful to protect yourself against negative influences. Even the conjunction can show a deep fear of dealing with the world.

If someone else brings his Neptune to you in a positive way, you could feel that you have known him for a thousand years. Past life or ancient connections are often felt. They could inspire you with their kindness and genuine support from the heart. This person can be a true friend or lover where the love between you runs very deep.

Neptune's negative effects on the Sun: A negative Neptune can lead us into difficult circumstances. A person with this pattern will have to exercise great will and develop a deep understanding of themselves to avoid self-destructive habits and actions. There is a tendency to associate with people who need their help because they were not supported by their father and now are trying to nurture the man back to health so he will love them. Women who do this are trying to heal the wounded bird. They attract men who are weak, wimpy, and wishy-washy because they have the need to "fix them up" and nurture them into wholeness. But it rarely works out that way.

If someone brings a negative Neptune to your Sun, he will sap your energy, appear other than he really is and deceive you in some way. He may cause you to deceive yourself because you will tend to see him other than he is. This kind of relationship is hard to figure out because there is always something illusive about it. But behind this illusive quality can be lurking a real deception. Even though you will really want to, don't believe anything this person tells you. Always check it out.

Neptune's positive effects on the Moon. This connection is very nurturing. A person with this combination, can be an extremely helpful person who really cares for other people. They are unusually sensitive to the emotional needs of others and show the deepest kind of caring. They are always there when people need their kind and comforting words. They are naturally attuned to the needs of others and have a deep sensitivity to their environment. They have a loving mother spirit. They like to create peaceful surroundings and may do a lot of meditating in their home as they are interested in spiritual matters. They have the power to attract very harmonious and benign forces into their life and often have a mysterious spiritual quality that people feel drawn to. They are naturally attuned to the subtle. Theirs is truly a caring heart.

If someone else brings you a positive Neptune you will feel their support right away. What they do for you tells you that they really do care. You will sometimes even feel healed in their presence. There can be a great bond between you and your connection may go beyond this lifetime. You will feel that this person really understands you.

Neptune's negative effects on the Moon. A person with this connection wears glasses of illusion. They tend to see the world the way they want to and are consoled by what might be or what they pretend to be. The difficulty is when reality knocks on their door. They have a great need for support and comfort because they were not sustained or nurtured as a child. They may look for this support in the wrong kind of people. The price they personally pay in money, energy and attention for that comfort may be too high. They often sacrifice themselves in situations with people who are not good for them. They will sometimes get swindled by those they trust. They tend to choose negative people who are not strong and who feed off of others.

If someone else brings you this kind of Neptune, then you may have to take care of their needs but your needs will not be met. You could feel obligated to this person for no apparent reason and they can make you feel guilty if you abandon them. They will usually bring out your need to help. But be cautious. They may be using you. As always with negative Neptunian influences, you have to work at keeping the situation out in the open and confront what is really going on. Any attempts to pretend or avoid the reality, should be confronted immediately so misunderstandings do not develop.

Neptune's positive effects on Venus. These positive patterns of Neptune exalt the energies of Venus. This person has unusual artistic abilities. Their imaginative wings can take them to places where they find remarkable inspirations. Whatever form of art they choose, they have the unusual capacity to make it the best. Musical tones or colors in painting can move the listener or viewer to profound feelings. They can communicate something of the sublime through their creative imagination. This position of Neptune also gives great love of friends and people in general and they are very supportive of others due to a deep sensitivity to other people's needs. They are full of romantic ideas and fantasy and are always seeking the absolutely perfect love.

If someone brings his Neptune to you in a positive way, you will consider them your dearest friend, as if you had always known them. Your love and friendship can extend far beyond any difference you may have between you. This is a relationship you feel will last forever regardless of what might really happen in life between you. Your love and friendship are deeper than most people and extend beyond this lifetime. This is something you will feel to be true.

Neptune's negative effects on Venus. If someone has this pattern (square), they tend to get involved in relationships that are full of complication and intrigue. One reason for this is that they tend to see in their friend or lover what they want to see rather than who they really are. Therefore, there is most always a real disappointment with friends and lovers when the reality of the relationship comes home. They may often find themselves being deceived by others either financially or emotionally because they trust them without question. Any devious person lurking in their life will reach out and take advantage of their trusting nature. Because of this, they feel abused and ripped off. The person with this pattern has a profound need to be loved and will often make great sacrifices just to get a little affection. But what a price to pay.

If someone brings your Venus a negative Neptune, you should be very cautious. They could be setting you up for a fall. This individual may promise you the sky but obviously can't deliver. You have to look at the potential karma of your relationship because another person's negative Neptune can distort your impression of him. He will stir your feelings of love and appear to be your friend, but if you invest your heart and time in him, expect to find something about him that you didn't know before. There can be a real sense of betrayal when the truth is finally known. This connection can generate craving for sexual ecstasy. But it can be treacherous because alcohol, drugs or perversion can be involved. The conjunction can show a form of entrapment. The person with the Mars can feel "sucked in" by the Neptune person. All illusions about the relationship should be confronted. Lovers will lie to each other.

Neptune's positive effects on Mars. If Neptune is related to Mars in a favorable way at birth, (sextile, trine and sometimes a conjunction), this person is born with a wonderful healing energy. Their effect on others can be very soothing. Others feel sustained and nurtured in this person's presence even without them doing anything. They are driven towards an ideal. They want to realize a creative goal. They would be outstanding as a physical therapist or counselor. People feel their warmth and are drawn to their company. They will be associated favorably with good people who are also very helpful and nurturing. They may relate to each other on a very deep level. Neptune's energy heightens the sexual energy, refines it and gives this person the capacity to relate to a lover in a very intimate way. If Neptune is conjunct Mars, they may be too idealistically attracted to those who need their help. Even with this positive energy, a person must be careful not to get drawn into a relationship that will be hard to dissolve. Neptune here can generate a kind of magnetic attraction that can be sexually very satisfying but also debilitating due to excess of appetite or craving.

If a person brings a positive Neptune to your Mars, they will be your dearest friend and possibly your greatest lover. They will always be there for you — ready to help when you need it. There is an opportunity to establish a very loving and deep connection between you that goes beyond the spoken words of "I love you." There can be something transcendental in your intimacy. Something that transports you both to a higher level of ecstasy. You may feel like you have known each other before. A familiarity that you cannot explain. These are often past life connections and are usually shown by Neptunian connections.

Neptune's negative effects on Mars: Since Mars is masculine in nature, a woman born with a negative relationship between her Mars and Neptune, will tend to see men through foggy lenses. She may imagine they are who they are not. She tends to attract men who take advantage of her because she lacks discrimination by associating with them. She could have martyr tendencies that make her a waiting victim. There is often a history of sexual abuse and deep-seated pains relating to childhood experiences with men. Neptune functions here as the robber or deceiver. This woman may often play the role of being used by men, and later find that this has always been her unconscious expectation. If she has been mistreated or rejected by men in her childhood, she may unconsciously expect to be the one who makes the sacrifices with the men she chooses. At some point, she must take a stand for her own goodness by walking away from those men who do not love her. At some point, she will get tired of having to be the one to fix up the relationship by always giving in to what the man wants. When she refuses to be with those men who don't love her and who do not give her their heart, she will begin to awaken to her own power as a woman. Great growth can come from this courageous gesture. It is a fire that will change her.

If a man brings your Mars a negative Neptune, then realize that he may try to seduce you through a beguiling romanticism. He can cause you to see him idealistically rather than realistically. Whatever he promises or proposes take with a grain of salt. Chances are he is not sincere and is only satisfying his own appetites. If you detect any deception or contradiction at all, you are probably right. Walk away and don't look back.

Neptune's positive effects on Mercury: This connection adds great inspiration to the mind. The mind lives in another world. The world of dreams, imagination, and creativity. Neptune reveals our desire for ecstasy. Therefore, this is an ecstatic mind. The thoughts are infused with subtle impressions of imagination, sound, words, or dreams. This is a wonderful pattern for a musician, artist, writer, or a silver-tongued orator. If this is your Mercury, you have been given a gift by the gods.

If anyone brings Neptune to your Mercury in a positive way, they can inspire your mind. Their mere presence has a calming effect on your thinking and you may perceive in them some kind of spiritual quality. This is an excellent connection for delving into the subtleties of life together. They will add intuitive inspiration to your thinking and help you find solutions to difficult problems.

Neptune's negative effects on Mercury: A person with this pattern has to be careful to tell the truth and not distort reality to suit his expectations. In some sense, it is a refusal to see the truth. There seems to be a deep fear of reality because it has been so painful in the past. This person could lie to himself or refuse to accept the facts. He can be woolly-minded and seem confused at times. Logical thinking is difficult for him because his unconscious fears distort his reasoning or perceptions.

If someone has his Neptune adverse to your Mercury, then you need to be careful in your communications. Often there is a lot of misunderstanding because the conversations are not clear or where unconscious assumptions take over and distort the messages. There may be disagreements over artistic and creative matters. Be careful to read between the lines if this person wants you to sign an agreement or contract. There may be something they are hiding. Keep your communications and agreements out front so no misunderstanding will develop. Remain on the cautious side.

PLUTO

Desire of the Soul

Not enough can be said about Pluto. It is a planet of such powerful, transforming energy that its fallout effects can last a lifetime. Pluto is the urge within us to move beyond our human existence, transcend our limitations, and express our heart's desire to merge with another — the Source. But this urge is so deep within our psyche that most of us are not aware of how to do this. Pluto is the "fire of Shiva." The God that destroys darkness and ignorance. That is, the energies of Pluto are trying to move us toward an open heart, but this energy is so intense that we often find it difficult to bear the pain of our own resistance to feeling such overwhelming love within us.

My own personal discovery of Pluto led me to the remarkable vision I described in the early part of this book. I discovered that a man's heart bears a feminine form and a woman's heart bears a masculine form. But beyond these lunar and solar energies, is the heart's essence, the soul. Pluto is our soul. Our purest and deepest desire. It is the core of our heart, beyond our masculine and feminine forms, and therefore Pluto is the deepest part of us. The heart seems to reflect the soul because the soul is the heart's desire. This is to say that the woman's heart (the Sun) reflects the soul, and the man's heart (the Moon) reflects his soul.

When you have planetary contacts with Pluto there is nothing ordinary in the energy expressed. When Pluto makes favorable contacts, all the great qualities of the soul and its capacity for the deepest love are expressed. When Pluto makes unfavorable contacts, its energies are thwarted and a tyrannical battleground may become the foreground of your life (crime, rage, and violence). It is extremely important to understand how Pluto is operating in your life. It holds the key to your ultimate freedom as a lover and as a creative human being.

Pluto's positive effects on the Sun: When we combine these two energies in a positive way (sextile, trine, and sometimes conjunction), we have one of the most powerful energy fields possible. A woman with the conjunction will demand more from life than she can possibly receive. She must find the answer from within herself and not demand it from the man she is involved with. A Plutonian conjunction sets up an unusual life situation for her. Even if her Sun is not negatively related to other planets, she will still look for absolute love from the man. In fact, she demands it from him. But at the root of this demand is a great fear. She was probably abandoned by her father or abused by him. Even if this did not actually occur, she was born feeling this way. Her compulsion is to make the outside man love her completely and absolutely. She has a deep disgust of weak men and she will be testing her lovers all of her life to see how strong they really are. She was born with a great sense of threat. A fear that something is going to happen if she does not protect herself. This makes her very demanding in close relationships. But what she must eventually realize is that the love she is looking for can only be found within herself. She cannot expect the man to be her strength. This love, as we have seen, can only be found within us. Perhaps she needs to ask a very important question: "Do I really want to stay in control of the relationship or am I willing to surrender my heart without seeking protection from loss?"

In the sextile and trine situation she has more capacity to love than anyone. This is a love that does not make demands. But, at the same time, she will not tolerate insincere relationships made up with phony games. She wants the ultimate love expression with her mate, but she will not make demands. She tends to give love to others and is not into control, but she does want her relationship to be deeply satisfying.

If someone brings you a positive Pluto, he could be the love of your life. If his Pluto is conjunct your Sun, this could truly be a past life connection and you could see your soul in the other person. You may be so connected to them that your love is greater than any other experience. If this is a man, he could be the "one you have always wanted".

Pluto's negative effects on the Sun: This person has a power struggle with life. They can be very aggressive and show a cruel streak because of very strong desires.

A woman with these patterns often shows great anger toward men and takes on an aggressive role in life. She may have been sexually abused. She can be very demanding and have a threatening quality that can frighten anyone. Her childhood usually shows abuse by the father or serious neglect. She has taken up the sword in defense against being ripped off. At the core of her heart she refuses to be vulnerable and lay down her sword. She has many painful memories that block her from being vulnerable to the male force, so she becomes that force in defense against it. This is a natural response for her to make, but she will never be happy with this position. She has a great potential for knowing what love really is, but she must cross over to surrendering her heart before she will discover her real power. She was born with a deep fear: the threat of being taken over, used, and abused. No matter how difficult it is, she must make the journey back to her man, because he holds the key to her true freedom.

If someone brings you a negative Pluto (usually square but sometimes a conjunction) you will feel threatened by them. They tend to make impossible demands on you which you feel you cannot possibly fulfill or refuse to submit to. However, they seem to have all the power, and you may feel compelled to give in just to keep the peace. But this is a one-sided concession and no real peace will come from it. You can never win in this situation because it will feel like they have a gun to your head. This relationship is a negative piece of karma, and you need to get yourself away from this situation as soon as possible. It could eventually turn violent. At some point, you may find yourself saying, "I'm not going to take this anymore."

Pluto's positive effects on the Moon: (Sextile and trine.) This position intensifies the feelings and relates closely to experiences with the mother, home, and family. There is a deep caring love nature that is very supportive and nurturing to others. Sensitivity is heightened and there is a psychic sense of the surroundings. This pattern lends greater awareness for the needs of others. Therefore, there is a natural inclination to help the homeless, the aging, the hungry, and the forsaken.

If another person's Pluto is related favorably to your Moon, they certainly would be your greatest support. They will always be there when you need them and will endure your hardships to help you through a crisis. Their connection to you can go beyond words. There is an unspoken love that endures through time.

Pluto's negative effects on the Moon: (This includes the conjunction.) This pattern presents a different picture all together. The conjunction and square are the most intense. The conjunction shows the loss of a nurturing connection to the mother. There is some form of abandonment. Even though the mother may not have literally abandoned this person, the individual feels like she did. There is a deep emotional fear that they will be forsaken.

This may not be conscious, but is played out in daily life. Therefore, with any hint or threat of loss of security, this person goes into panic. They are intensely emotional and very demanding in getting their emotional needs fulfilled because they are driven by fear and anxiety.

If another person relates to your Moon in this way, you will feel very threatened by them. One man, whose wife had her Pluto square his Moon, "felt like she had a gun to my head". They make intolerable demands upon the Moon person. This is definitely a pattern to avoid in a relationship. It is very difficult to live under and it is hard to say "no" to the Pluto person because of the threatening quality of their demand.

Pluto's positive effects on Venus: This increases the love nature and desire for a quality relationship. There is little tolerance for casual or shallow love affairs. This person is deeply loyal in his/her affections and looks for real substance in love. The intense energy of Pluto exalts the desire of Venus and shows that they have a deep love nature. Because of this sensitivity and refinement of feeling, there can be remarkable expressions of beauty through art.

If someone has his Pluto relating to your Venus in this way, you will feel a deep connection to him. He may feel like an old friend, someone you feel totally relaxed with. If his Pluto is conjunct your Venus, this can add a compulsive quality to your relationship. He could be obsessed with you and possibly take you into ecstasy. Even though this is a very strong connection, it is important to watch your feelings closely to avoid entrapment. In some cases, this connection can bring the deepest love and friendship possible between two people. These connections are often experienced as love at first sight.

Pluto's negative effects on Venus: A conjunction can drive this person to be very demanding in matters of love and be very manipulative in getting what they want.

They want the heart and soul of their lover and their friends, and require a great deal of attention. There may have been loss of the mother or an experience of abandonment at an early age. If other planets relate favorable to this conjunction, the compulsive demands based on a deep fear of loss, may not be as deceptive in fulfilling its emotional needs. The square pattern also works in demanding ways. This person will find it difficult to be truly vulnerable because of an inherent fear of rejection and loss. While they expect a lot from love, they find it difficult to give someone else their heart without a solid guarantee.

Obviously, if someone has his Pluto negatively related to your Venus, they will make compulsive demands upon you. If it is a man, he will be obsessed with you. But be careful to see if this is real love or possession. Sometimes lovers with this connection may have been together in a past life and have come together again to complete their relationship. Beware of being coerced into a relationship that you instinctively know is not good for you. It will be difficult to break the connection once it has been established.

Pluto's positive effects on Mars: A person with this pattern (sextile and trine) has a great deal of drive and sexual energy. There is usually a strong will in evidence and they have an amazing capacity to endure many hardships. They know how to use energy effectively and can be extremely creative. But Pluto here primarily moves the passions. A woman with this favorable position can threaten men because of the intensity of her desire. But no harm is intended. The desire is great. If it is a conjunction, she can challenge men to take her if they can handle her. She is fiercely attracted to strong men who can match her intensity. She is a fighter or champion of causes and may have had an intense relationship with her father.

If a man's Pluto falls on your Mars, you could be in for an intense sexual relationship. This is passion in its highest state. You could become obsessed with your desire for him and may not be conscious that the relationship may not be about love but about lust. It is very difficult to refuse to engage this affair because it goes deeper than a mere romance. This energy will really spin your chakras!

Pluto's negative effects on Mars: This is a pattern of intense feeling that can be very threatening to others. There is a capacity for violence if the energy is triggered in the wrong way. A woman with this configuration may have been sexually abused as a child. She could be full of great rage and carry a weapon, ready to emotionally castrate any man who is too weak to stand up to her. She can be very challenging and have a desire for confrontation. Anyone else with these positions can basically be very aggressive and often find themselves in situations that can be quite dangerous. This is a very volatile pattern, especially if it is a square configuration (90 degrees).

If a man has his Pluto related negatively to your Mars, be careful of your relationship. He will want to take you over, take control of your life, and be in charge. This connection is so intense that you have to be very careful not to play out negative and compulsive games with him. You will be fascinated by this person because he is able to reach the depths of your desire, but it is still a fiercely possessive energy. Negative reactions could be the result. This could be pure lust.

Pluto's positive effects on Mercury: This pattern imparts to the individual a very keen mind. The mind works like an X-ray. President Clinton has this pattern and he has mentioned that the mind has to be like a laser. There is great perception and deep understanding of any subject the mind wishes to focus on. The energies of Pluto intensify the mind's capacity to see into things. This is a detective's mind — a mind that can ferret out the truth from a bundle of lies. There can be a great capacity for research and penetrating the causes of things. These people can be great writers, speakers or researchers because they go directly to the issues that matter. Their mind can be threatening because they tend to have a penetrating gaze that can make others feel naked or uncomfortable in their presence.

If someone has Pluto related to your Mercury in a positive way, they can certainly help you reach the depths of your thinking and challenge you to look deeper. You may feel like you have learned a lot in their company because they can actually help you awaken a new awareness of things. At times, you may feel pressured in their company but you will usually find it is a positive and beneficial association.

Pluto's negative effects on Mercury: This individual has a very coercive mind. They know what they want when they want it and tend to project this demand upon others. It is as if they were obsessed with their ideas, documents, writings, or papers. They seem to have a deep fear that something awful will happen to their communications. Fear drives them to make impossible demands upon other people. They have a very keen intellect but it is expressed in such a negative way that other people avoid them. Most people who work with this individual will feel threatened by their anger or intensity of demand.

If someone has his Pluto adversely related to your Mercury, you will have a terrible time trying to please them. They will place such exacting demands upon you that you will begin to act strange and insecure. You will become plagued with trying to second-guess what this person wants. If they are your boss or superior, ask for a transfer because you will never be able to please them, and whatever you do for them will never be good enough. They will make you feel inadequate and stupid, when you obviously are not. If you continue the association, you will only make more mistakes and matters will get worse. Get away as fast as you can. This could fester into a serious communication problem.

10

Table of Personal Planets

Listed below are additional relationship possibilities that you may want to consider after comparing the transpersonal planets with your personal planets. Try these after you have had some experience with the previous information.

His/ Your	Your/ His	Connected in a Harmonious Way	Connected in a Discordant Way
SUN	MOON	Increases Comfort	Uncomfortable
	VENUS	Social and Sexual Pleasure	None
	MARS	Enterprising/Energy	Obstruction
	MERCURY	Agreements	None
MOON	VENUS	Comfort and Pleasure	Indulgence/Selfishness
	MARS	Emotional Fervor	Anger/Frustration
	MERCURY	Enhances Communication	Confuses Communication
VENUS	MARS	Intense Passion	Sexual Frustration
	MERCURY	Social/Artistic Harmony	None
MARS	MERCURY	Intense, Creative Communications	Arguments

11

The Plutonian Process

The mysterious process of the heart and its awakening can be discovered through personal encounters with the planet Pluto. "What does this mean?" If you practice the principles laid out in Part I of this book, you will discover true intimacy and awaken your heart to love. But the majority of people may have great resistance to taking this journey. It is a very direct path, quite intense, and offers no room for "taking time." If you are a woman and were born between February 20-25 (Pisces 0 to 5 degrees), May 22-27 (Gemini 0 to 5 degrees), August 24-29 (Virgo 0 to 5 degrees, or November 24-27 (Sagittarius 0 to 5 degrees) your heart is going to be opened by the powerful planetary energies of Pluto starting in 1995. I say "women" because it is their Sun in these degrees of the solar energy fields that will be affected. Since the Sun is the heart of a woman (male), she will go through profound emotional changes toward men. (See **Schedule of Pluto's Visits** on page 198.) What does Pluto have to do with this? Pluto represents a spiritual force that opens the heart into intense feeling. We cannot resist its power to affect us. It is a most unusual and remarkable planet. It is an energy that radiates from the core of our being — our very soul. Men born during the above periods will be affected differently. Their desire to achieve and break away from stagnant conditions will be intensified. They often display a remarkable will power or break away from an intolerable situation.

When Pluto is in a frustrating relationship to our personal planets by conjunction or square we are terrified that we will be cut off from our own source. There is a deep sense of threat that something terrible will happen if we don't protect ourselves or demand what we need. This is an overt reaction and very unreasonable because we live in an unconscious state of terror that we may be ripped off at any moment. We can be very unreasonable, demanding, and selfish. Because of the intense fear, a person with heavy Plutonian patterns is required out of emotional necessity to concentrate on his own needs so strongly that he will often overlook the needs of others.

If you have Pluto in relationship to any of your personal planets, you will be intensely related to those things these planets represent. As we have seen, if Pluto is conjunct your Venus, you will place intense demands upon your lover and those people you are close to. If they make the same demands on you, you will recoil and resent it. If Pluto is adverse to your Mars, you will be domineering and unreasonable. If Pluto is conjunct your Moon, you will feel emotionally abandoned by your mother and have great fear of the future. You will have no sense of home. If Pluto is trine your Venus, you can be the greatest of lovers because you love deeply. But as a **visiting** planet, Pluto can change your life forever.

Pluto As a Visiting Planet

A visiting planet is one that is presently moving in the sky and makes a contact with one of our birth planets just as another person's planet makes contact with ours. The real Plutonian Process occurs when Pluto becomes a visiting planet in our life. What kind of effect does Pluto have upon us as a visitor?

If Pluto hits one of the emotionally tender zones in our planetary patterns (where the Sun, Moon, Venus or Mars are adversely related to Saturn, Uranus, Neptune, or Pluto from birth) it can be a very devastating planetary episode. None of our neurotic patterns of manipulation will work any more. We can't get people to do what we want them to do and we have to confront all the pain that has been suppressed by our fears of childhood. As a visiting planet, Pluto will dig up every thing related to our neurosis. This intense drama is usually played out with other people. There can be great weeping, rejection, loss of lover, no support, and deep alienation from others. Those close to us do not understand what is happening because they have no basis from which to advise us. We are turned in upon ourselves and are forced to feel all the feelings we have hidden from ourselves. Our skin may burn, our bones may ache, and our heart may break. This appears to be a terrible thing to happen to us, but it is actually a blessing because Pluto does not let up until something has been changed within us for the better. It is a magical fire that consumes us and forces us to feel our own heart. If we engage this Plutonian Process consciously — embrace it and be willing to go through it — we will be reborn into love. It will teach us what love is. We will awaken to love for ourselves and for others and attract the one who was meant to be with us because we make a place for them in our own heart, or our relationship to our present lover will be totally transformed for the better. This is what happened to Son of the Eagle.

Son of the Eagle is a well-known rock star who was a very different man before his Plutonian Process. His wife describes their relationship before the transformation:

"Before Pluto came along, Eagle was out of touch with his feelings. When I would go through some emotionally bad times, he would try to understand and feel

what I was feeling, but it didn't work. I never quite felt his support emotionally. He just couldn't connect. He held everything inside and was not able to say how he felt about his emotions. He was afraid of his feelings. At the time, I thought we were very close, but it was only later after the process that we discovered our greatest love for each other.

Before his transition, he was Mr. Nice Guy who went along with people even though they were taking advantage of him. He was afraid to be honest in his feelings with other people. When he started going through the Pluto transition, he became very angry at me, himself and the world. His career almost came to a dead halt and everything seemed to be falling apart. He would sometimes tremble because the fear of the unknown was so great. He went through two years of anxiety attacks, crying, and feeling's of intense terror at times. He felt as if he was drowning and couldn't catch his breath. During this time, I became pregnant and we were running out of money. He felt like a failure. He was afraid I would leave him and he felt unworthy of my love. He said he didn't deserve to be loved.

But now, he is a totally different man. He can relate on a much deeper level because he has been through so much emotionally. His feelings are more intense and his heart has opened up. He is much more whole as a person. He has a lot more compassion, and is more thoughtful and loving. But the biggest change I have noticed is that he is very honest and true to himself, and, therefore, he is no longer afraid of people and standing up for himself. He speaks the truth and follows his heart."

What was it that caused all of Eagle's agony and eventual transformation? It was Pluto. Visiting Pluto passed back and forth over his Venus at 17 degrees of Scorpio for about two years. At the time of his birth, his Saturn was less than 10 degrees from an exact conjunction to his Venus in Scorpio. (See **Saturn's negative effect on Venus**, pages 146-147.) So we can see that he was born with a psychic hole in his heart — a profound sense of emptiness, rarely feeling good about who he was. Venus is the goddess of his heart and she was held in bondage all of her life by Saturn, the Scrooge of the sky. Saturn gave her the fear of coming out and being known. She was sensitive to being hurt so she stayed in her cell of fear. But Pluto killed Saturn, who was Venus' only defense against intimacy. So there she stood raw, naked, and defenseless. She could no longer hide behind Saturn's strategies of avoiding intimacy. Eagle had no choice but to feel his loss totally; his loss of love and support from his inner feminine. She could not help him because she was not allowed to feel and to be known. She was held in bondage by the control of Saturn. But when Saturn was shattered by Pluto, Venus came out into the light and became known. This was an excruciating experience for Eagle. He never allowed himself to feel so deeply. As a result, he became a changed man emotionally. His goddess was set free. He became more of a man because the nurturing power of the goddess was released from within him. His woman finally emerged from his heart. He now has the emotional freedom and strength to make the decisions he feels are right for him as a man. Pluto awakened his Venus from bondage and set his feelings free. His only price was to totally feel his sorrow and his loss and embrace the goddess. It took great courage for him to go through this fire of the heart. Fortunately, he had a loving wife to help him feel through it to the other side. This was his Plutonian Process. Now, his wife has a new husband. A heart-awakened man.

    I recently heard him play. I was totally moved in my heart by his music. Son of the Eagle is rising once again to take his place among the stars.

Even if we do not have any frustrated personal planets from birth, if Pluto visits one of them, the Plutonian Process will still occur. Although it may have less external drama, Pluto's impact will still be felt on a very deep level.

The Plutonian Process is one of the ways that will open our heart and our body to true intimacy. But it does not come to everyone. If you have personal planets in the energy fields of Scorpio, Taurus, Leo, and Aquarius, you have already been introduced to the fire of Pluto and fully understand the meaning of feeling. You may have already had a chance to make the journey to your own power as a lover because Pluto compels us to feel the deepest parts of ourselves.

A woman can discover that her heart is a man and a man can discover that his heart is a woman. When Pluto makes his visit, this is the time for this awakening to occur. This is the chance to discover this wonderful secret. To have this vision.

To repeat, beginning in 1995 and 1996, Pluto enters the first degrees of the solar field of Sagittarius which will bring the opportunity for intense love experiences for those women born between February 20-25, May 22-27, August 24-29 or November 24-27. (See **Schedule of Pluto Visits** on page 198 to determine where Pluto will be in the next two years.) Also, any man or woman born with personal planets in the first 5 degrees of the Sagittarius, Gemini, Virgo, or Pisces energy fields may have similar emotionally transforming experiences. In fact within the next 13 years, these four energy fields of the Sun will be under the transforming power of Pluto. If you have personal planets in these fields, you should eventually come to know the Plutonian Process — an opportunity to engage the awakening of your heart. If a man has his Venus or Moon in these fields, he will be confronted with the fire of the feminine. He will have to feel his own depths and face the "awe of the goddess." This is what happened to me when I described my experiences in the opening section of this book.

12

Basic Effects of Visiting Planets

The visiting planets reveal the kind of events that will come from the outside world. Since other people are usually involved in bringing these events, we should always look at our present relationships when interpreting the meaning of these visiting planets. We can then get a very good idea of what is happening. When one of these planets is approaching within one degree of the conjunction, sextile, square, or trine, it is near the point of occurrence.

For example, a friend asked about her chances of having a man in her life. I glanced at the position of her birth planets and checked the visiting planet Mars (male). I saw that visiting Mars was approaching her birth Uranus within one and a half degrees on November 9th and reaching exact by November 13th. On November 9th, she went out to a party with some friends, had a good time, but nothing happened. The next day, she said she was discouraged and didn't think anything was going to happen. I said, "But November the 12th and 13th are not here yet. Mars will be right on your Uranus then. Just wait. Something surprising will occur. If it doesn't, I will be the most surprised of all. Because Uranus is involved, this could show a sudden love experience." She called me on November 12th and told me the man she had a crush on called her and asked her out. She was totally surprised because he had not shown that much interest in before. Her faith in planetary chemistry has certainly been renewed.

An event often comes about when the relationship is exact, but it may occur before this time or slightly after. You will need to experiment with your planetary energies to determine your own timing.

Jupiter. Jupiter is the least significant of the five visiting transpersonal planets. Because he travels faster than the rest of them, his impact is not as great. But you can look to Jupiter to bring positive connections to other people and a chance to expand your opportunities.

If Jupiter forms a positive relationship to your planets, look for a chance to grow and to have positive experiences in your life. Use the meaning of Jupiter and the interpretations starting on page 138 to determine what effect it might have on your personal planets. Then look to your present relationships to see who might represent Jupiter. If its effect is negative, read the section relating to Jupiter and the planet involved for your interpretation. As an example, if Jupiter makes a positive or negative contact with Mercury it would affect your thinking, plans and communications in some way because Mercury relates to these matters. See pages 141-142. See Jupiter's Visits on page 189 for Jupiter's schedule.

Saturn. Saturn's visit to one of your planets always brings a teaching experience into you life. He is always teaching us lessons. Some of these we feel we can do without, but we are given the lessons anyway! Even when Saturn forms a positive relationship with our personal planets, there is usually a serious quality to the experience. For example, we may receive a promotion, but will have to take on a lot more work. Saturn usually has this "**yes, but**" quality. "**Yes**, I got a promotion, **but** now I have a lot more pressure to handle."

See the Saturn section on page 142 for your interpretation and page 193 to find the dates when Saturn will visit one of your birth planets. Again, your interpretation must be based on whether you have positive or negative patterns to the planet that Saturn visits. It is important to remember that "negative" does not always mean bad. The energies are simply difficult to work with. Great strength of character can often be developed through such experiences. It all depends on your response to the demands these forces represent.

Uranus. Uranus is a very volatile and unpredictable planet. When it visits another planet, it can bring sudden changes. Uranus seems to take a personal planet by the neck and move it wherever it wants to take it. For example, if Uranus conjuncts your Venus or Mars there can be a sudden romance or sexual encounter. If it forms a square to Mars, there could be a sudden accident, sexual abuse, or fight with a man. Again, it depends on how this is set up in the chart. If the well-known football player, O.J. Simpson, was born in the early morning, he would have his Moon square Uranus at birth, which would account for a hair-trigger temper in relationship to women. (See pages 151-152 which describes this pattern.) Was this Moon/Uranus pattern under planetary stress on June 12, 1994?

If you have stressful planets to Uranus at birth, you may have a short fuse. If Uranus comes into contact with this stress zone, it is time to practice relaxation, get away from stressful situations, and try to compromise with others. Look at pages 196-197 to determine where Uranus will be in the next three years.

Neptune. Neptune is a very subtle planet. Its energies are not very obvious, but are definitely experienced on the emotional and subconscious level. If Neptune's visit is positive, he will bring sublime feelings, a lifetime lover, creativity, and divine inspiration. If negative, beware of deception, intrigue, dissipation, or loss of strength and power. Beware of trying to escape from life through drugs, alcohol, or sexual excesses. The escape tendency can be very strong, so beware of the tendency of not living up to your promises or shirking responsibility. Certainly other people may not live up to theirs during this time. See pages 156-163 for descriptions of the positive and negative effects of Neptune for your interpretation.

Pluto. See page 174 for a detailed description of Pluto as a visiting planet.

For a "hands on" experience of the basic effects of visiting planets, let us use the one degree approaching as the point to begin our timing. Look to see what transpires from that point until the time when the planet reaches an exact relationship. I will walk you through the procedure.

If you look at your own computer printout, you will see at the top of the chart to your right a column of planets with the degree and solar field of each planet listed. (I hope you have ordered your chart!)

Please turn to page 69 to see how the computer chart on page 68 was translated into a simple wheel. Make sure the solar energy fields of your blank wheel (which you can draw by hand) matches the solar energy fields of the computer printout of the wheel. It is important to remember that everybody's wheel will print out differently due to date, time, and place of birth. For instance, notice that Libra 180 degrees marks the first energy field on the left and all the other fields follow in sequence. Ignore the actual numbers outside the computer wheel printout, e.g., the 0 degrees and 31 minutes of the solar energy field of Libra, and so on. Use the actual degrees of the circle that mark each energy field as was done in the translated chart. In our example chart, Libra starts at 180 degrees of the circle, Scorpio starts at 210 degrees, Sagittarius starts at 240 degrees, and etc. If the first field on the left in your printout is Pisces, then you start with 330 degrees. The next energy field would be marked off at 360 degrees (or 0 degrees of Aries) since you are back at the beginning of the 360 degree circle. Mark off the rest of the fields in their natural sequence and put your computer readout planets in their appropriate energy fields. This is not as complicated as it appears in writing. All you have to do is put the planets in the correct energy field as shown by the computer readout.

Let us assume that you want to see if any transpersonal planet is visiting your Moon in a positive or negative way. Go to the **Table for Visiting Planets** on pages 186-187 and copy these pages for easy reference. Keep these at your side. Let us say that your computer chart shows that your Moon was at 5 degrees of Virgo when you were born. Look at the **Table for Visiting Planets** and find the Virgo Solar Field in the first column on page 186. Note that Scorpio, Capricorn, Pisces, Taurus, and Cancer are in harmony with the Virgo Solar field and that Sagittarius and Gemini are discordant. Now, let us assume that you want to know how Pluto is affecting your Moon, which would be your emotions, habits, relationship with women, home, and family. Turn to the **Schedule of Pluto's Visits** on page 198. Note that Pluto is in Sagittarius 0 to 6 degrees from January 17, 1995 to January 8, 1998. You can already see that sometime during this period Pluto will form a square to your Moon because Sagittarius is 90 degrees away from Virgo and therefore discordant (see the discordant energy field opposite Virgo in the **Table for Visiting Planets**). We want the dates when Pluto is within one degree of square (4 degrees of Sagittarius) and when it is exactly square (5 degrees of Sagittarius). The **Schedule of Pluto's Visits** shows us that Pluto was at 4 degrees:

Dec 26, 1996 - Jan 21, 1997
Apr 24, 1997 - Jun 2, 1997
Oct 20, 1997 - Nov 15, 1997

Read **Pluto's negative effect upon the Moon** on pages 166-167. These are the most intense periods of Pluto's effect upon the Moon (your security, home, family, habits, childhood memories, and emotions). This effect is negative in the sense that it does not feel good, but the final result can be very beneficial because Pluto always has a transforming effect on our lives. It is a purger and a purifier of gross and blocked energies. You will be very conscious of this intensity during this time and can gain a great deal of understanding of your emotions and your experiences as a child. For a man, this can be a great transformation of his heart, because it is so strongly connected to the mother principle (Moon). If you already have planets that have difficult planetary patterns to your Moon (square and sometimes conjunctions), then you will certainly have the test to understand and resolve your frustrations. A contact by Pluto can trigger some unfinished business. This would be a time to change all of that and bring it to an end. If you have favorable planetary patterns, the intensity will not be as great, but Pluto will still strongly affect your life in those areas I have mentioned. Let us look at another planet. (Since planets go forward and backward, Pluto's effect can be around as long as two years. It makes sure the work is completed.)

Let us say that your Sun is at 3 degrees of Aquarius. Look at the **Table for Visiting Planets** and find the Aquarius entry in the first column on page 187. Notice that Aries, Gemini, Leo, Libra, and Sagittarius are harmonious fields and Taurus and Scorpio are discordant. If you look over the Pluto planetary schedules on page 198, you will see that Pluto enters Sagittarius on January 17, 1995. This energy is in harmony with your Sun and will help you realize your goals. See **Pluto's positive effects on the Sun,** pages 164-165. For a woman, this can bring a very loving relationship into her life, or make relationships with men (Sun) very graceful and harmonious. Pluto is forming a sextile relationship with your Sun (the woman's heart) which is positive. Now, let us look for other connections.

On February 16, 1996, the planet Uranus is at 2 degrees of Aquarius and will reach the 3 degree point on March 7, 1996. (See **Schedule of Uranus' Visits** on page 196.) This is a conjunction. If you have favorable planetary energies to your Sun at birth, you will become very creative, original, and independent during this period. You may also suddenly (Uranus) meet a man (Sun) and fall in love. This is only one of the many possible interpretations. What will be felt generally is the urge to be yourself, to try new things, and to break away from stagnant and unproductive conditions in your life. If you have unfavorable planetary energies relating to your Sun at birth (e.g. Saturn, Neptune, or Pluto conjunct or square your Sun), you will still break away from old conditions and try new things but there will be a lot more drama involved. There could be some very intense confrontations with others at this time. But these encounters may be necessary to give you a greater understanding of how you react to others.

Jupiter will also be making a conjunction to the Sun at 3 degrees of Aquarius on February 4, 1997. Notice how fast Jupiter moves. It is at 2 degrees and 12 minutes on January 31 and in four days has already reached the 3 degree point. This shows that Jupiter's effect does not stay around very long. This visit could simply indicate a few nice days with men friends, enjoying their company and having a good time. As I have said before, do not expect great things from Jupiter. He often promises a lot, but does not deliver very much unless other planets are lending their support at the time he comes around for a visit.

TABLE FOR VISITING PLANETS

Solar Field	Harmonious Energy Fields	Discordant Energy Fields
Aries	Gemini Leo Libra Sagittarius Aquarius	Cancer Capricorn
Taurus	Cancer Virgo Scorpio Capricorn Pisces	Leo Aquarius
Gemini	Leo Libra Sagittarius Aquarius Aries	Virgo Pisces
Cancer	Virgo Scorpio Capricorn Pisces Taurus	Libra Aries
Leo	Libra Sagittarius Aquarius Aries Gemini	Scorpio Taurus
Virgo	Scorpio Capricorn Pisces Taurus Cancer	Sagittarius Gemini

BASIC EFFECTS OF VISITING PLANETS

Solar Field	**Harmonious Energy Fields**	**Discordant Energy Fields**
Libra	Sagittarius Aquarius Aries Gemini Leo	Capricorn Cancer
Scorpio	Capricorn Pisces Taurus Cancer Virgo	Aquarius Leo
Sagittarius	Aquarius Aries Gemini Leo Libra	Pisces Virgo
Capricorn	Pisces Taurus Cancer Virgo Scorpio	Aries Libra
Aquarius	Aries Gemini Leo Libra Sagittarius	Taurus Scorpio
Pisces	Taurus Cancer Virgo Scorpio Capricorn	Gemini Sagittarius

13

Schedule of Visiting Planets

SCHEDULE OF JUPITER'S VISITS 1995 – 1997

Solar Field	Degrees	Dates
Sagittarius	5°	Jan 3, 1995 - Jan 7, 1995
		Jul 17, 1995 - Aug 20, 1995
	6°	Jan 8, 1995 - Jan 12, 1995
		Jul 3, 1995 - Jul 16, 1995
		Aug 21, 1995 - Sep 3, 1995
	7°	Jan 13, 1995 - Jan 18, 1995
		Jun 23, 1995 - Jul 2, 1995
		Sep 4, 1995 - Sep 12, 1995
	8°	Jan 19, 1995 - Jan 23, 1995
		Jun 14, 1995 - Jun 22, 1995
		Sep 13, 1995 - Sep 20, 1995
	9°	Jan 24, 1995 - Jan 29, 1995
		Jun 6, 1995 - Jun 13, 1995
		Sep 21, 1995 - Sep 27, 1995
	10°	Jan 30, 1995 - Feb 5, 1995
		May 29, 1995 - Jun 5, 1995
		Sep 28, 1995 - Oct 4, 1995

Jupiter in Sagittarius (cont'd)

11°	Feb 6, 1995	- Feb 12, 1995
	May 21, 1995	- May 28, 1995
	Oct 5, 1995	- Oct 10, 1995
12°	Feb 13, 1995	- Feb 20, 1995
	May 13, 1995	- May 20, 1995
	Oct 11, 1995	- Oct 16, 1995
13°	Feb 21, 1995	- Mar 2, 1995
	May 2, 1995	- May 11, 1995
	Oct 17, 1995	- Oct 21, 1995
14°	Mar 3, 1995	- Mar 17, 1995
	Mar 18, 1995	- May 1, 1995
	Oct 22, 1995	- Oct 26, 1995
15°	Mar 17, 1995	- Apr 17, 1995
	Oct 27, 1995	- Oct 31, 1995
16°	Nov 1, 1995	- Nov 5, 1995
17°	Nov 6, 1995	- Nov 10, 1995
18°	Nov 11, 1995	- Nov 15, 1995
19°	Nov 16, 1995	- Nov 19, 1995
20°	Nov 20, 1995	- Nov 24, 1995
21°	Nov 25, 1995	- Nov 29, 1995
22°	Nov 30, 1995	- Dec 3, 1995
23°	Dec 4, 1995	- Dec 7, 1995
24°	Dec 8, 1995	- Dec 12, 1995
25°	Dec 13, 1995	- Dec 16, 1995
26°	Dec 17, 1995	- Dec 21, 1995
27°	Dec 22, 1995	- Dec 25, 1995
28°	Dec 26, 1995	- Dec 29, 1995

SCHEDULE OF VISITING PLANETS

Jupiter in Sagittarius (cont'd)

29°	Dec 30, 1995 - Jan 3, 1996	

Jupiter in Capricorn

0°	Jan 4, 1996 - Jan 7, 1996
1°	Jan 8, 1996 - Jan 12, 1996
2°	Jan 13, 1996 - Jan 16, 1996
3°	Jan 17, 1996 - Jan 21, 1996
4°	Jan 22, 1996 - Jan 25, 1996
5°	Jan 26, 1996 - Jan 30, 1996
6°	Jan 31, 1996 - Feb 4, 1996
7°	Feb 5, 1996 - Feb 9, 1996
	Aug 24, 1996 - Sep 14, 1996
8°	Feb 10, 1996 - Feb 14, 1996
	Sep 15, 1996 - Oct 1, 1996
9°	Feb 15, 1996 - Feb 20, 1996
	Jul 28, 1996 - Aug 6, 1996
	Oct 2, 1996 - Oct 11, 1996
10°	Feb 21, 1996 - Feb 25, 1996
	Jul 19, 1996 - Jul 27, 1996
	Oct 12, 1996 - Oct 19, 1996
11°	Feb 26, 1996 - Mar 2, 1996
	Jul 11, 1996 - Jul 18, 1996
	Oct 13, 1996 - Oct 26, 1996
12°	Mar 3, 1996 - Mar 8, 1996
	Jul 3, 1996 - Jul 10, 1996
	Oct 27, 1996 - Nov 2, 1996
13°	Mar 9, 1996 - Mar 15, 1996
	Jun 24, 1996 - Jul 2, 1996

Jupiter in Capricorn (cont'd)

14°	Mar 16, 1996 - Mar 23, 1996	
	Jun 17, 1996 - Jun 24, 1996	
	Nov 9, 1996 - Nov 13, 1996	
15°	Mar 24, 1996 - Apr 1, 1996	
	Jun 7, 1996 - Jun 16, 1996	
	Nov 14, 1996 - Nov 19, 1996	
16°	Apr 2, 1996 - Apr 14, 1996	
	May 16, 1996 - Jun 6, 1996	
	Nov 20, 1996 - Nov 24, 1996	
17°	Apr 15, 1996 - May 25, 1996	
	Nov 25, 1996 - Nov 29, 1996	
18°	Nov 30, 1996 - Dec 4, 1996	
19°	Dec 5, 1996 - Dec 8, 1996	
20°	Dec 9, 1996 - Dec 13, 1996	
21°	Dec 14, 1996 - Dec 18, 1996	
22°	Dec 19, 1996 - Dec 22, 1996	
23°	Dec 23, 1996 - Dec 26, 1996	
24°	Dec 27, 1996 - Dec 31, 1996	
25°	Jan 1, 1996 - Jan 4, 1997	
26°	Jan 5, 1997 - Jan 8, 1997	
27°	Jan 9, 1997 - Jan 13, 1997	
28°	Jan 14, 1997 - Jan 17, 1997	
29°	Jan 18, 1997 - Jan 21, 1997	

SCHEDULE OF SATURN'S VISITS 1995 – 1997

Solar Field	Degrees	Dates
Pisces	8°	Jan 2, 1995 - Jan 12, 1995
	9°	Jan 13, 1995 - Jan 22, 1995
	10°	Jan 23, 1995 - Jan 31, 1995
	11°	Feb 1, 1995 - Feb 9, 1995
	12°	Feb 10, 1995 - Feb 17, 1995
	13°	Feb 18, 1995 - Feb 25, 1995
	14°	Feb 26, 1995 - Mar 5, 1995
	15°	Mar 6, 1995 - Mar 14, 1995
	16°	Mar 15, 1995 - Mar 22, 1995
	17°	Mar 23, 1995 - Mar 30, 1995 Nov 20, 1995 - Nov 24, 1995
	18°	Mar 31, 1995 - Apr 8, 1995 Oct 19, 1995 - Nov 19, 1995 Nov 25, 1995 - Dec 25, 1995
	19°	Apr 9, 1995 - Apr 17, 1995 Oct 3, 1995 - Oct 18, 1995 Dec 26, 1995 - Jan 9, 1996
	20°	Apr 18, 1995 - Apr 27, 1995 Sep 20, 1995 - Oct 2, 1995 Jan 10, 1996 - Jan 20, 1996
	21°	Apr 28, 1995 - May 8, 1995 Sept 6, 1995 - Sep 19, 1995 Jan 21, 1996 - Jan 31, 1996
	22°	May 9, 1995 - May 20, 1995 Aug 24, 1995 - Sep 5, 1995 Feb 1, 1996 - Feb 9, 1996

Saturn in Pisces (cont'd)

23°	May 21, 1995 - Jun 6, 1995	
	Aug 6, 1995 - Aug 23, 1995	
	Feb 10, 1996 - Feb 18, 1996	
24°	Jun 7, 1995 - Aug 5, 1995	
	Feb 19, 1996 - Feb 26, 1996	
25°	Feb 27, 1996 - Mar 5, 1996	
26°	Mar 6, 1996 - Mar 13, 1996	
27°	Mar 14, 1996 - Mar 22, 1996	
28°	Mar 23, 1996 - Mar 30, 1996	
29°	Mar 31, 1996 - Apr 7, 1996	

Saturn in Aries

0°	Apr 8, 1996 - Apr 15, 1996	
	Nov 13, 1996 - Dec 24, 1996	
1°	Apr 16, 1996 - Apr 24, 1996	
	Oct 24, 1996 - Nov 12, 1996	
	Dec 25, 1996 - Jan 12, 1997	
2°	Apr 25, 1996 - May 3, 1996	
	Oct 11, 1996 - Oct 23, 1996	
	Jan 13, 1997 - Jan 25, 1997	
3°	May 4, 1996 - May 13, 1996	
	Sep 27, 1996 - Oct 10, 1996	
	Jan 26, 1997 - Feb 5, 1997	
4°	May 14, 1996 - May 25, 1996	
	Sep 14, 1996 - Sep 26, 1996	
	Feb 6, 1997 - Feb 14, 1997	
5°	May 26, 1996 - Jun 7, 1996	
	Aug 30, 1996 - Sep 13, 1996	
	Feb 15, 1997 - Feb 23, 1997	

SCHEDULE OF VISITING PLANETS

Saturn in Aries (cont'd)

6°	Jun 8, 1996 - Jun 27, 1996
	Aug 10, 1996 - Aug 29, 1996
	Feb 24, 1997 - Mar 4, 1997
7°	Jun 28, 1996 - Aug 9, 1996
	Mar 5, 1997 - Mar 12, 1997
8°	Mar 13, 1997 - Mar 20, 1997
9°	Mar 21, 1997 - Mar 28, 1997
10°	Mar 29, 1997 - Apr 5, 1997
11°	Apr 6, 1997 - Apr 13, 1997
12°	Apr 14, 1997 - Apr 22, 1997
13°	Apr 23, 1997 - Apr 30, 1997
	Nov 24, 1997 - Jan 8, 1998
14°	May 1, 1997 - May 9, 1997
	Nov 4, 1997 - Nov 23, 1997
15°	May 10, 1997 - May 18, 1997
	Oct 22, 1997 - Nov 3, 1997
16°	May 19, 1997 - May 28, 1997
	Oct 10, 1997 - Oct 21, 1997
17°	May 29, 1997 - Jun 8, 1997
	Sep 27, 1997 - Oct 9, 1997
18°	Jun 9. 1997 - Jun 22, 1997
	Sep 12, 1997 - Sep 26, 1997
19°	Jun 23, 1997 - Jul 12, 1997
	Aug 23, 1997 - Sep 11, 1997
20°	Jul 13, 1997 - Aug 22, 1997

SCHEDULE OF URANUS' VISITS 1995 – 1997

Solar Field	Degrees	Dates
Capricorn	25°	Jan 1, 1995 - Jan 10, 1995
	26°	Jan 11, 1995 - Jan 27, 1995
		Sep 3, 1995 - Nov 9, 1995
	27°	Jan 28, 1995 - Feb 13, 1995
		Aug 4, 1995 - Sep 2, 1995
		Nov 10, 1995 - Dec 5, 1995
	28°	Feb 14, 1995 - Mar 5, 1995
		Jul 10, 1995 - Aug 3, 1995
		Dec 6, 1995 - Dec 25, 1995
	29°	Mar 6, 1995 - Apr 1, 1995
		Jun 10, 1995 - Jul 9, 1995
		Dec 26, 1995 - Jan 12, 1996
Uranus in Aquarius		
	0°	Apr 2, 1995 - Jun 9, 1995
		Jan 13, 1996 - Jan 29, 1996
		Sep 11, 1996 - Nov 8, 1996
	1°	Jan 30, 1996 - Feb 15, 1996
		Aug 10, 1996 - Sep 10, 1996
		Nov 9, 1996 - Dec 6, 1996
	2°	Feb 16, 1996 - Mar 6, 1996
		Jul 16, 1996 - Aug 9, 1996
		Dec 7, 1996 - Dec 27, 1996
	3°	Mar 7, 1996 - Apr 1, 1996
		Jun 16, 1996 - Jul 15, 1996
		Dec 28, 1996 - Jan 13, 1997
	4°	Apr 2, 1996 - Jun 16, 1996
		Jan 14, 1997 - Jan 30, 1997
		Sep 20, 1997 - Nov 8, 1997

Uranus in Aquarius (cont'd)

5°	Jan 31, 1997 - Feb 17, 1997	
	Aug 17, 1997 - Sep 19, 1997	
	Nov 9, 1997 - Dec 9, 1997	
6°	Feb 18, 1997 - Mar 4, 1997	
	Jul 23, 1997 - Aug 16, 1997	
	Dec 10, 1997 - Dec 29, 1997	
7°	Mar 9, 1997 - Apr 2, 1997	
	Jun 25, 1997 - Jul 22, 1997	
	Dec 30, 1997 - Jan 16, 1998	
8°	Apr 3, 1997 - Jun 24, 1997	
	Jan 17, 1998 - Feb 2, 1998	
	Sep 28, 1998 - Nov 9, 1998	

SCHEDULE OF NEPTUNE'S VISITS 1995 – 1997

Solar Field	Degrees	Dates
Capricorn	22°	Jan 1, 1995 - Jan 12, 1995
		Sep 6, 1995 - Nov 2, 1995
	23°	Jan 13, 1995 - Feb 8, 1995
		Jul 24, 1995 - Sep 5, 1995
		Nov 3, 1995 - Dec 12, 1995
	24°	Feb 9, 1995 - Mar 13, 1995
		Jun 14, 1995 - Jul 23, 1995
		Dec 13, 1995 - Jan 9, 1996
		Sep 28, 1996 - Oct 15, 1996
	25°	Mar 14, 1995 - Jun 13, 1995
		Jan 10, 1996 - Feb 5, 1996
		Aug 2, 1996 - Sep 27, 1996
		Oct 16, 1996 - Dec 7, 1996

Neptune in Capricorn (cont'd)

Degrees	Dates
26°	Mar 6, 1995 - Apr 1, 1995
	Feb 6, 1996 - Mar 7, 1996
	Jun 25, 1996 - Aug 1, 1996
	Dec 8, 1996 - Jan 5, 1997
27°	Mar 8, 1996 - Jun 24, 1996
	Jan 6, 1997 - Feb 1, 1997
28°	Dec 4, 1997 - Jan 2, 1998

SCHEDULE OF PLUTO'S VISITS 1995 – 1997

Solar Field	Degrees	Dates
Sagittarius	0°	Jan 17, 1995 - Apr 21, 1995
		Nov 10, 1995 - Dec 11, 1995
		Jun 20, 1996 - Sep 28, 1996
	1°	Dec 7, 1995 - Jan 2, 1996
		May 14, 1996 - Jun 19, 1996
		Sep 29, 1996 - Oct 30, 1996
	2°	Jan 3, 1996 - Feb 15, 1996
		Mar 27, 1996 - May 13, 1996
		Oct 31, 1996 - Nov 25, 1996
		Jul 20, 1997 - Sep 7, 1997
	3°	Feb 16, 1996 - Mar 26, 1996
		Nov 26, 1996 - Dec 21, 1996
		Jun 3, 1997 - Jul 19, 1997
		Sep 8, 1997 - Oct 19, 1997
	4°	Dec 26, 1996 - Jan 21, 1997
		Apr 24, 1997 - Jun 2, 1997
		Oct 20, 1997 - Nov 15, 1997
	5°	Jan 22, 1997 - Apr 25, 1997
		Nov 16, 1997 - Dec 11, 1997
	6°	Dec 12, 1997 - Jan 8, 1998

14

Listening to the Voices of the Planets

When we hear of someone who "hears voices" we may think they are a little crazy, or perhaps psychic or clairvoyant. But the fact is that all of us hear voices. They are the internal dialogues that we carry on within ourselves all the time. For example, "Should I continue to go to school or should I get a job?" Another part of you may answer, "I better not quit now. I'm too close to the end. But what if I fail? I can't. I've got to keep trying." It may not seem so, but different parts of ourselves are asking and answering these questions all the time.

That part of you that has an intense desire to succeed may be in conflict with another part that actually wants to fail. Or, in another situation, you may have a strong attachment to a particular man but also want to be free from any commitment. These voices are expressing conflicting desires. The internal dialogues we carry on with ourselves most of the time can be understood as the voices of the planets within us. We explored this briefly in Chapter 8. Now, we will analyze these voices in greater depth and become very clear on what they are saying. Let us take a close look at our planets and the patterns they form with each other. What do the deeper parts of ourselves want and need? What do they really mean? We need to listen to the Sun's voice, the Moon's voice, and all the other planetary voices.

Usually, no planet speaks with a pure voice because it is influenced by the desires of the other planets around it. So, what we learn to listen to is our own unique mixture of voices. Our internal planetary dialogues. Let us look at a few examples from my files. Only the names of the individuals are fictitious.

Example 1. Venus Square Mars. Dana's Venus is in Scorpio and her Mars is in Aquarius. Notice that Scorpio is water (see pages 54 and 55 for a description of Scorpio) and Aquarius is air (see page 56 for a complete description of Aquarius). Now look at page 171 which describes Venus and Mars when in a discordant relationship to each other (square) as **sexually frustrating**. Water and air are not compatible. It is obvious that these two energy fields do not get along. Their desires are manifested as voices in conflict. They are square each other (90 degrees apart). The Key Phrase for Venus in Scorpio, pages 109-110, is **"I love the mystery of sex, the joy of intensity, loyalty in love and being with one person."** Now if we take the Key Phrase of Mars in Aquarius from page 125 we get **"I desire independence, sexual freedom, and the right to explore."** We can see immediately that these two meanings are in conflict. The table on page 187 also shows us that the Scorpio solar field is discordant with Aquarius. The basic inner conflict is between Dana's desire for independence and sexual freedom and loyalty in love and being with one person. Let us expand this logic by looking further at her situation.

Dana has a deep love and great passion for Robert, her lover, but she also likes to have a lot of male friends. She wants to "keep" Robert (Venus in Scorpio) but also wants sexual freedom (Mars in Aquarius). The conflicting desires show us that she wants Robert for herself but also wants to keep these other men in her life. She may not realize that this creates a conflict until she sees Robert with another woman. Her Venus in Scorpio energies arouse her anger, suspicion, and jealousy toward Robert because she is very possessive of him. If she tells him about her feelings, he may bring up the fact that she is always going out with other men, so why shouldn't he go out with other women. She is trapped because she knows it is true, but she may try to defend herself by saying "Yes, but they are just friends. Not lovers." Robert may reply "Well, the other women I go out with are also just friends. Looks to me like you want your cake and eat it too."

Example 2. Moon Square Pluto. Helen's Moon is in Cancer and her Pluto is in Libra. While we do not have any description for Pluto in the solar energy fields, we can understand the problem immediately if we look at **Pluto's negative effects on the Moon**, pages 166-167.

This is a pattern that shows Helen was abandoned (Pluto) emotionally by her mother (Moon). She feels internally that she was never nurtured and as a result always lives in an unconscious fear that she will be abandoned again. Even though her mother may have never abandoned her physically, Helen will still feel as if she did emotionally. Here we see Pluto as an energy that is blocked by the Moon, but since Pluto is a much more powerful planet, the Moon side (sense of being nurtured, fed and sustained) is the part that feels threatened. Here is usually the way this pattern is played out with others: Helen has a great emotional desire to relate intimately with others but she tends to make intense demands upon those she is close to. She can be domineering and hard to please because she lives with an unconscious fear that something can happen at anytime to rip her off.

For example, she may ask her husband if he paid the rent and he casually answers. "No. I forgot. I'll do it tomorrow." She goes into an emotional rage. "Don't ever do that again. The owner will kick us out, and before you know it, we will be living on the streets." In the past, he used to tell her what he thought about her reactions, but now he only shrugs his shoulder and says to himself, "That's Helen. Always in a panic." When someone makes demands on her, she resents it and feels burdened by their desires. Her desire to be free of obligation is in conflict with her intense desire for love, protection and guaranteed security. She has a deep need for love but may have a hard time giving it without placing a lot of conditions and guarantees on the other person. She feels bound by a deep fear of abandonment and is in doubt of ever being nurtured.

Example 3: Mercury Conjunct Uranus. Now, let me walk you through your own analysis of Mercury conjunct Uranus. Mercury is in Taurus. If it is conjunct Uranus, Uranus is also in Taurus. The question is, "Is this positive or negative?" The answer is if Mercury is not afflicted (squared) by another planet, the energy is positive. If you look at pages 50-51, you will see a concise description of the Taurus energy field. Taurus is an earthy and materialistic energy. With Mercury here, it shows that the mind is focused on material acquisition and achievement of a practical nature. Now if we put the powerful electrifying energy of Uranus with Mercury what do we get? A mind that is very creative with practical things. See the description of Uranus on pages 149 and 150 and the positive effect of Uranus on Mercury on pages 154 and 155.

An Exercise With Saturn Conjunct Venus

Now it is your turn to do one on your own. What would be the effect of a man's Saturn conjunct a woman's Venus? I will give you a start by saying that this is a negative pattern. Read the following paragraph after you have made your own discovery and compare.

LISTENING TO THE VOICES OF THE PLANETS

I will wait for you here.

Did you turn to the **Contents** at the beginning of the book and look up Saturn's positive and negative effects in Chapter 9? **Saturn's negative effects on Venus** are found on pages 146-147. The description of this pattern will enlighten you enough to know that you do not want this relationship. If you ever run into this pattern in your own life, you will quickly understand what I mean. This is a red flag signal. Do not try to get this person to love you. You will be wasting your time.

More Examples of Planetary Effects

To find your own planetary voices, you will need to determine where all your planets are and how they relate to each other. You will need your date, time and place of birth ready to put into the computer. Then your planetary patterns can be determined by calculating the position of the planets at the time of your birth. **(There are several options for obtaining your own planetary patterns which are described on page 221. If you have not ordered your birth patterns, please do so now.)**
To do these calculations by hand is time-consuming so we have computer programs to do them for us. If you have a computer readout of your planetary patterns, you can see how I am analyzing this chart. If not, it is still easy to follow. Let us learn how to look at these patterns. See **Chart A** on the next page.
The birth information of a young woman — we will call her Jana — was put into our Mac computer using a *Skyclock* program. The upper part of this printout is generated by the program and we will translate this information and transfer it to our empty wheel as shown in **Chart A.**

203

Chart A - Jana's Childhood

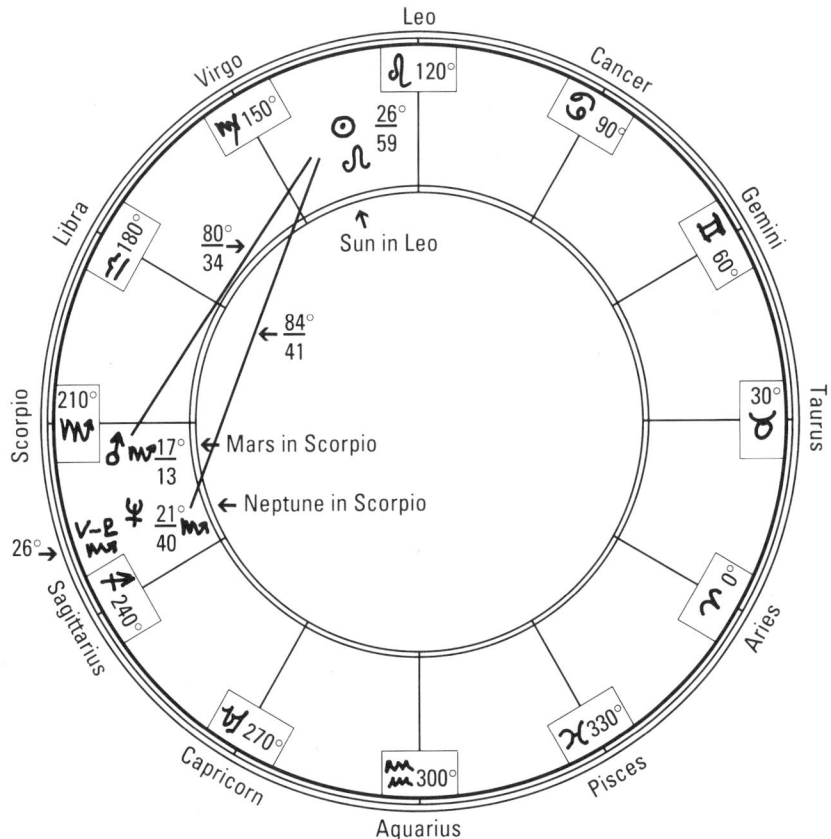

If we look closely at the major planetary patterns involved in **Chart A** above, we can see the source of Jana's feelings. Notice how her male energies (Mars and the Sun) are frustrated from birth. Mars is conjunct Neptune which shows that her male energy was undermined or made fearful through deception from a man or men. (Neptune can be the greatest deceiver. See page 161 to get this information on Mars conjunct Neptune. Remember that a conjunction is a negative contact since these planets are also square to the Sun in the pattern.) Since Mars in a woman's chart is her urge for intimacy, that urge is often sealed in fear if she has been abused by a man as a child. It is difficult for her to be vulnerable later in her intimate relations as an adult. Here, Neptune's conjunction weakens Mars and manifests as deep sexual anxieties. It is also afflicting the Sun by square.

In the past, Jana looked at men through dreamy eyes because it was painful for her to feel the true relationship of abuse and manipulation she was subjected to as a child. To survive emotionally, she had to imagine a more harmonious world for herself. As a result, she created fantasies and impossible relationships that had no chance for true intimacy. She often met men who abused or used her in some way, and since she had not processed the pain that was still locked in her memories, she was still attracting these negative types. She often gave herself to men even when she did not want to because she would rather have some hope of love than have none at all.

After many years of analyzing this pattern, I have discovered that Neptune conjunct Mars for a woman in almost every case shows sexual abuse (deception [Neptune] by a male [Mars]). Even the time when this abuse happened to Jana can also be determined. Notice that Mars at birth was 4 degrees and 27 minutes from exact conjunction to her Neptune. It is traditional to move a planet by progression one degree for a year of life. So, when Jana was four-and-a-half years Mars made its conjunction to Neptune by this form of measurement. I asked Jana if it was okay to explore her childhood. She said, "Yes, by all means. Tell me what you see." I asked her if she ever had any memories of sexual abuse. (It looked like this had actually happened around four-and-a-half years of age.) "Oh, God! Yes. I'm just now getting in touch with that." Notice also that Jana's Sun at 26 degrees and 9 minutes of Leo is only 5 degrees and 19 minutes from exact square to Neptune. Since the heart of a woman is revealed by her Sun—her sense of goodness and strength—I said her power had been undermined by Neptune (the planet of no support) in her fifth year. This feeling of no support may have been triggered by the sexual abuse and worsened by Neptune later in her fifth year. (The real solution to these feelings could possibly be reached gradually through regressive hypnotherapy by helping her relive her past if she was ready to do so.) This Sun square Neptune pattern says "no support from the father" because Neptune weakened the Sun, Jana's heart. This pattern most always indicates that the father was an alcoholic or abandoned his children. This was absolutely true in Jana's case. She confirmed that her father was an alcoholic. But, fortunately, a new life has emerged for her. She has experienced the Plutonian Process, and is already emerging as a beautiful, heart-awakened woman.

Note the **V-P26** in the Scorpio energy field next to Neptune. This shows that visiting (V) Pluto is at 26 degrees of Scorpio (P26) and is forming a square relationship with her Sun (nearly 91 degrees apart). Pluto first came into a square contact with her Sun on December 29, 1993. What does this mean? It was the beginning of "the awful truth." She said, "I felt there was no love for me anywhere." This is often the kind of experience we have when Pluto visits our personal, feeling planets. This was my own personal experience as well as that of Son of the Eagle. (Review the **Plutonian Process** in Chapter 11 for a deeper understanding.)

Chart B - One Man's Emotional Patterns

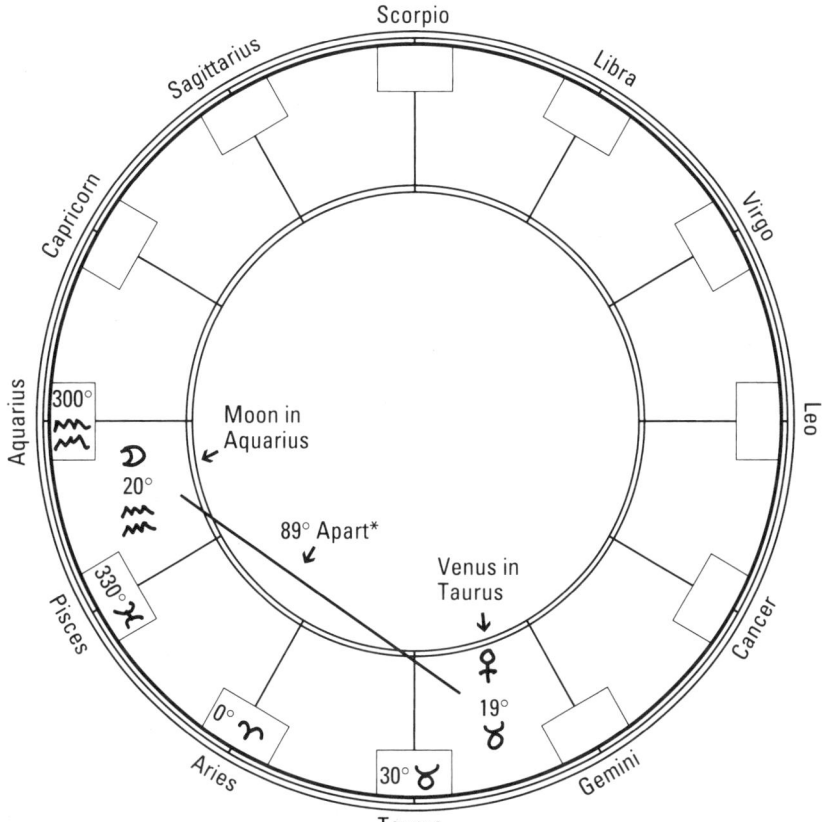

* Since the Moon is moving faster than Venus, it is one degree less than 90° exact. However, this is not a fact that will affect your interpretation. You only need to understand that both planets are within the orb of a square.

Let us look at another example of planetary effects in **Chart B** to show how to read the emotional nature of a man. Let us assume that you have just met this man and you are attracted to him and want to know what he likes in a woman. The two planets that will tell you the most about his emotional nature — his inner woman — are his

Moon and Venus. This is the kind of woman he will look for in the outside world. Once you have analyzed how these needs are expressed within him, you can determine if you fit into his expectations. (I cannot overstress the importance of these two planets in regards to discovering how a man really feels about a woman and what his emotional attitudes are towards her.) Let us listen to the voice of his feminine planets.

As you can see, his Moon is in Aquarius at 20 degrees square his Venus at 19 degrees Taurus. (I have omitted his other planets for the sake of clarity.) Although the two planets are 89 degrees apart, they are within the "orb" of influence. What is he looking for in a woman? With his Moon in Aquarius, he is comfortable and secure in having many women friends. (See pages 99-100.) Here, the voice of the man's Moon is saying, "I like to have a lot of women friends around me. The choices fascinate me. I like all the possibilities of being with them. I like this kind of freedom with women. The freedom to choose those women I want to be with at any given moment." But the voice of Venus sings a different song. She says, "I like just one woman. I don't want to share her with anybody. I expect her to be true just as I am true." As you can see, these are needs in strong conflict with each other, conflicting voices. They will create serious emotional complications for this man in his relationship to a woman. He wants his lover to be true, but at the same time he demands personal freedom to explore his own sexual possibilities with other women. One woman, whose husband had a similar planetary combination, was so frustrated that she told him to go find a prostitute. "You need a wild whore," she said. "You don't know how to relate to a real woman."

As you can see, having this kind of information before you go into a relationship can help you understand what a man really wants from you. You are in an excellent position to make an intelligent decision. Of course, your intuition could tell you the same thing, but when we become emotionally involved with someone, it is difficult to see them clearly. Even though we may lie to ourselves about someone we care about, you can rest assured that the planets will not lie to you. They will tell you what is going on inside of a person. What they are really like.

Another example: a man who has his Saturn conjunct a woman's Sun (within 10 degrees plus or minus of her Sun in the same solar field) would always be criticizing her and she would feel it. (See page 144 for a description of Saturn's negative effects on the Sun.)

I once analyzed the charts of a couple who had so much going for them in their relationship except for this difficult Saturn/Sun pattern. I told them this could be "the fly in the ointment" — the one thing that would give them trouble. I told the man that if he could give up his criticism of her, they could make it together. But no matter how hard he tried, he could not. She eventually left him because she could no longer endure being reminded of what he saw as basic defects in her character. So, whom do you blame? No one. Their chemistry was almost perfect together, but this was a crucial planetary pattern. Saturn is the authority figure and the Sun is her heart. It could not work out with his critical, controlling energy repressing her heart energy. He criticized her very being. Her personal actions aroused his displeasure. Another woman would not affect him this way. Another man who does not have Saturn on her Sun, may not find any fault in her. In fact, he could love the very things in her that the Saturn man despised.

During the writing of this book, a woman came to me and asked about her relationship to her lover. I told her "You have a strong connection to each other and there is no doubt that there is a deep love here. But there is one problem that would test your relationship." "What is that?" she asked. "Do you recognize that part of him that gets into weeping and wailing and says 'poor little me'?" She said,

"Yes, I do." I told her "His Saturn is right on top of his Venus which shows that he was not loved in his childhood and that he does not feel sustained inside by his inner woman. He looks in the outside world for the woman who will supply that nurturing. He will tend to place his need for love and nurturing upon you. But your Saturn is exactly square his Venus so you cannot stand that quality in him. In this pattern, you play the part of the critic and see his complaint as weak and wimpy." "That's true," she said. "I want to pounce on him for being that way." I said, "Right now you are not living together. What do you think it would be like if you were?" "Worse," she replied. I told her they could not have a mature relationship until he had processed his own pain by becoming truly vulnerable and discovering his own feminine strength from within. I told her he would have some major emotional confrontations with his needs in two years when the visiting planet, Saturn, made a conjunction with his Venus. "Do I have to wait that long," she asked. "You might," I replied. "That's something you have to consider."

In another situation, a man's wife loves his spontaneous poetry and inspires him to be humorous, but a former wife saw him as stupid for "trying to be funny." Knowing what he does now about planetary energies, he certainly would not have engaged that relationship. She had her Pluto square his Moon. (See pages 166-167.)

These observations lead us to the obvious conclusion that we need to learn how to make the right choice to begin with and avoid the strain and pain of divorce altogether. This is living in wisdom.

15

Read This Before Getting Married

It has been suggested by some authorities that trial marriages are good for people in their 20s — just to test out relationships. This seems to be what is happening. The Census Bureau reports that in 1992 nearly one-and-a-half million young adults between 25 and 29 years of age were divorced. But "trial-and-error" marriages would be totally unnecessary if people would explore their planetary chemistry together. Instead of sociologists or marriage counselors trying to understand why marriages break up, it would be far more beneficial to help each person understand who the other person really is.

Premarital counseling is basically useless if the counselor does not know the inner nature of each person he or she is trying to counsel. The planets can reveal this information immediately to a trained observer. If all counselors were required to learn about the planetary energies that are transmitted between people, they would never again hear the complaint, "I thought he was different. He is just not the man I thought he was when I married him."

If we use the ordinary tools of insight, they are simply not enough. They will fail most of the time. We simply do not know a person by what they present to us because they are often quite different on the inside than the outside. This adds complexity to the nature of any person, but if we understand their planetary patterns, we can understand their inner life. I do not know of any attitudes, desires, and motivations of a person that can be more easily understood than by looking at the planetary chemistry that was formed at the time of their birth.

Since the planets reveal who we are, we can find out in just a few minutes whether a relationship will really work or not. This is because we are working with real energies between people, not theories, beliefs, statistics, studies, or our assumptions. The following example will illustrate this process. (Do not let all the lines and symbols confuse you. We will dissect each segment one at a time and your understanding will become quite clear.)

Chart C - Brief Portrait of a Relationship

HIS		HERS
☽ 11 ♏ 23	Moon	☽ 17 ♑ 08
☉ 10 ♉ 01	Sun	☉ 21 ♋ 00
☿ 21 ♉ 59	Mercury	☿ 15 ♌ 04
♀ 24 ♓ 33	Venus	♀ 00 ♍ 17
♂ 02 ♋ 54	Mars	♂ 13 ♍ 48
♃ 21 ♊ 17	Jupiter	♃ 18 ♎ 42
♄ 29 ♉ 01	Saturn	♄ 27 ♋ 29
♅ 29 ♉ 11	Uranus	♅ 19 ♊ 34
♆ 27 ♏ 28 ℞	Neptune	♆ 06 ♎ 02
♇ 03 ♌ 31	Pluto	♇ 10 ♌ 48

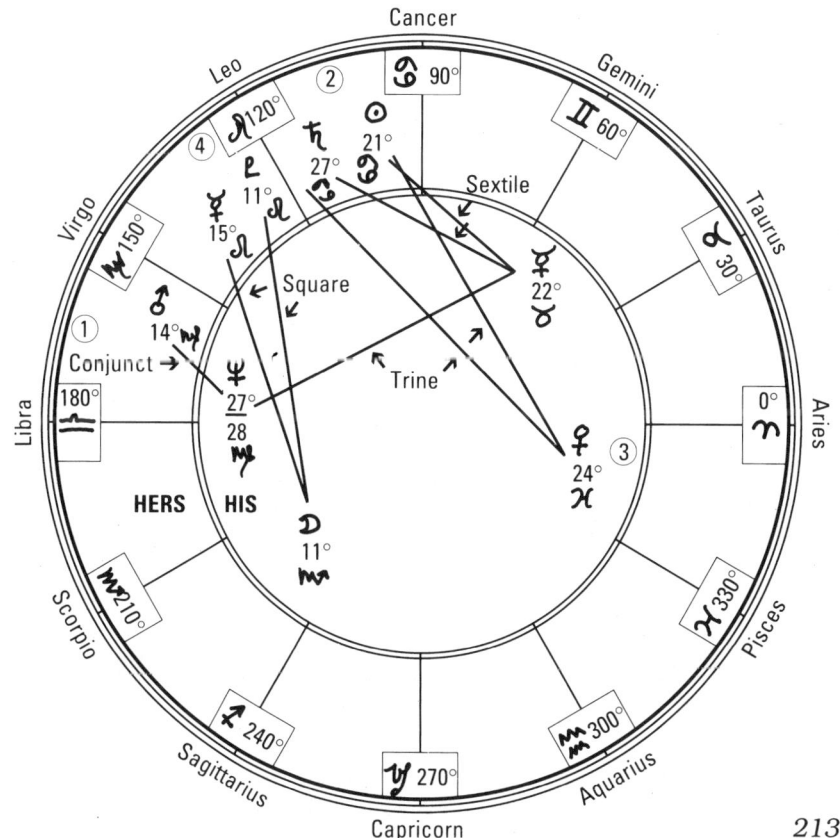

Chart C shows the major relationship patterns between a man and a woman already married. The inner wheel of the chart shows his planets, hers are on the outside. Look at the relationship pattern "1" circled next to her Mars in Virgo at 14 degrees. Even though the Mars conjunction to Neptune is a little wide, it is still operative. Because of this pattern, I knew they had a deep love for each other and figured they knew each other in some previous time. (See **Neptune's positive effects on Mars**, pages 160-161.) I said, "When you first met, you felt like you knew each other right away. Is that right?" "Oh, yes," the woman replied. "It was uncanny. It was like we didn't need to get to know each other at all."

Let us look at the relationship pattern at number "2" circled on the chart next to her Sun and Saturn. Note that the Sun and Saturn energies in Cancer relate favorable by sextile (60 degrees apart) to his Mercury at 22 degrees Taurus. This is a very cooperative communication line that works well together to produce results. Taurus and Cancer attitudes (energy fields) cooperate nicely to build a nest together. (See the second paragraph in the **Saturn's positive effects on Mercury**, pages 148-149.) Now go to the number "3" next to his Venus on the sample chart. Note that her Sun and Saturn are trine to his Venus, so you would read the favorable section for these planetary combinations. Number "4" on this chart shows that her Pluto and Mercury are square to his Moon. Her Mercury conjunct her Pluto gives her a very intense and demanding mind, sometimes intolerant of others. This energy is adverse to his Moon. Although there is a lot of harmony and beneficial qualities in this relationship, this is still a very difficult pattern to work with.

If a single woman knew she had Pluto in Leo in an adverse relationship to her lover's Moon in Scorpio, and had studied this book, she would know why she should think twice before marrying this man. She would know that her fiery, impulsive go-getting Pluto would always be after the slothful, couch-potato habits of the man who has his Moon in Scorpio. She would be extremely irritated and frustrated by what she sees as his "laid-back, lazy habits." But he, on the other hand, would probably complain that "It feels like she's always got a gun to my head. There's no peace. I can't relax." This was the exact description I gave to this couple and they were shocked at how accurate it was. I told them they had to work to compromise this energy; that it was difficult for both of them to live under. They will probably stay together because they have other redeeming, harmonious energies in their relationship, but I usually consider this a red flag for a woman or man going into such a relationship. However, we must realize that neither person is at fault. No blame is intended. It is simply a planetary mix that does not work well together.

Generally, people whose Pluto squares or conjuncts our personal planets seem to feel that they need to change us in some way. They will work on a fault they see in us as if it was a disease and elect themselves as the master surgeon who is going to cut it out. They pounce on this flaw and remind us of our failures. That is the unrelenting quality of Pluto.

Planetary pressure imposed upon us by another person can bring out the worst in us. Anger and even hatred can arise from the depths of a basically harmonious person when they are pushed against the wall. Certain individuals with very stressful planets to ours can make us feel the worst of feelings. This is why it is extremely important to know what the planetary energies are between us and another person before we engage in a serious relationship with them. A person with this kind of energy in relation to ours is the person we have never wanted. We must stay away from them. They can bring absolute misery into our life. Again, this does not mean that the Pluto person is bad. They are simply bad for us.

If we put the Pluto-in-Leo person and the Moon-in-Scorpio person with someone else, these separate planetary energies may not function negatively in that relationship. For example, if a woman's Pluto in Leo forms a trine to a man's Moon in Aries, she would experience him as a fiery active male and would be much happier with him. He is certainly no couch potato. But none of us can erase how we were born. To blame either person is like cursing a cake for turning out wrong when we use nail polish as a basic ingredient.

16

The Master Table

Degrees of Solar Field	Solar Field Symbol	Name and Dates	Element
0 - 30	♈	Aries 3/21-4/19	Fire
30 - 60	♉	Taurus 4/19-5/20	Earth
60 - 90	♊	Gemini 5/20-6/21	Air
90 - 120	♋	Cancer 6/21-7/23	Water
120 - 150	♌	Leo 7/23 - 8/23	Fire
150 -180	♍	Virgo 8/23 - 9/23	Earth
180 - 210	♎	Libra 9/23 -10/23	Air
210 - 240	♏	Scorpio 10/23 -11/23	Water
240 - 270	♐	Sagittarius 11/23 - 12/21	Fire
270 - 300	♑	Capricorn 12/21 - 1/19	Earth
300 - 330	♒	Aquarius 1/19 - 2/19	Air
330 - 360	♓	Pisces 2/19 - 3/21	Water

THE MASTER TABLE

Positive/Negative Attitudes	Planetary Ruler	Planetary Areas Ruled by the Planet
Aggressive, fearless, unyielding initiator	Mars	Fire, iron, surgical instruments, knives, spears, guns, war, masculinity
Slow, tenacious, persistent, materialistic, stubborn, and sensual	Venus	Banks, idealism, femininity, relationship, marriage and partnerships
Witty, versatile, light-fingered, impatient, dishonest, and crafty	Mercury	Communication, transportation, letters, contracts, neighbors, and mental activity
Sensitive, imaginative, moody, protective, security-minded, and crabby	Moon	Stomach, grocers, chefs, bakeries, houses, mother, silver, habits, family, and security
Proud, independent soft-hearted, dramatic, and egocentric	Sun	Gold, children, theatres, entertainment, heart, ego, speculation, and gambling
Serving, neat, critical, analytical, and efficient	Mercury	Small animals, employees, health, work and service
Social, artistic, indecisive, harmonious, and wishy-washy	Venus	Marriage, partnership, public relations
Intense, jealous, proud, cautious, vengeful, and secretive	Pluto	Death, regeneration, mysteries, taxes, insurance, sexuality, and the occult
Restless, blunt, bigoted, aspiring, hard worker, truthful	Jupiter	Publishing, law, foreign countries, churches, long trips, ministers, philosophy, higher education
Practical, ambitious, austere, cold, stingy, honest, limited spirituality	Saturn	Bones, real estate, knees, business, government, tradition, responsibility
Ingenious, unpredictable, opinionated, indifferent, detached	Uranus	Television, computers, airplanes, telephones, high-tech, planetary psychology, electricity, higher awareness
Impractical sympathetic, artistic, creative, dreamy escapist, sacrificial	Neptune	Hospitals, drugs, alcohol, gas, ocean, music, poetry, meditation, monasteries and prisons

17

How to Obtain Your Planetary Patterns

The Easy Way

• You can receive a computer readout of your birth patterns and translate them yourself by using this book. The benefit of this is the actual experience of finding and understanding your planetary patterns or those of another person. (The technical data required to obtain your planetary patterns is too costly and complex to include in this book. That's why this simple ordering system is the easy way.) Please send date, time, place of birth, a self-addressed, stamped envelope, and $3 to cover data input and handling for each person to Amrita Publications, P.O. Box 2008, San Anselmo, California 94979. (You can mail cash if you prefer not to bother with a $3 check.) If time is unknown, sunrise will be used. Copy the Form from page A-7 of the Appendix and fill out the appropriate section(s).

• You can receive a computer readout of your birth patterns with a translation of symbols and energy fields as a study guide. Patterns are listed with appropriate page numbers where they can be found in this book. Please send date, time and place of birth, a self-addressed, stamped envelope, and $6 for each person to Amrita Publications, P.O. Box 2008, San Anselmo, California 94979. If time is unknown, sunrise will be used. Copy the Form from page A-7 of the Appendix and fill out the appropriate section(s).

- If you want us to compare your planets with someone else, you can use the comparison as a study guide as we explain how we reached our conclusions. This is a way for us to share our insights with you and to clarify your understanding. It is a learning tool for matching up relationships. Please send date, time, place of birth, a self-addressed, stamped envelope, and $30 for a comparison for two to Amrita Publications, P.O. Box 2008, San Anselmo, California 94979. If time is unknown, sunrise will be used. Copy the Form from page A-7 of the Appendix and fill out the appropriate section(s).

The Challenging Way

If you wish to learn how to do everything yourself, you will need to purchase a table of houses, an ephemeris, an atlas, and a beginner's handbook. All of these can be purchased through ACS, P.O. Box 34487, San Diego, CA 92163-4487 or your local metaphysical or occult book store (approximate cost $100). You may also try AFA, Inc. at 6535 S. Rural Road, P.O. Box 22040, Tempe, Arizona 85282 (602) 838-1751. They will send you a catalog of books and/ or list of software. You may also find these books in your local library.

Appendix

Further Adventures In Planetary Chemistry

The following workshops are conducted each year throughout the United States. If you would like to set up a workshop in your area and attend for free, write to:

>Randall Curtis
>Amrita Publications
>P.O. Box 2008
>San Anselmo, California, 94979

NATIONAL WORKSHOP PROGRAM

Workshop A: Discover and Actualize What You Were Born To Do

What is your true purpose for being here? Learn how the planet, Pluto, shows your reason for being born and how it reveals your true heart's desire. Discover that desire, verbalize it, and know where and how to actualize it in your life.

Explore your greatest talents and abilities. Discover how your particular combination of planets create the internal voices that lead the way to your true gifts. You will find these internal voices in your birth patterns, and explore them, and learn how to use them creatively.

Overcome your "assumed" limitations. The planet, Saturn shows a pattern of assumed limitations from birth (inherited karmic lessons not yet resolved). By inducing altered states of consciousness, you can access this area and change it. By listening to your Saturn voice, you will understand your assumptions and limitations and learn to navigate through your subconscious mind. We do not accept the limitations of Saturn as if we were condemned to live them out forever, but since they are usually assumed unconsciously from birth (a karmic inheritance of unresolved experiences of the past), we need to make these attitudes more conscious and change them into creative activities.

Experience altered states of consciousness. Learn new techniques for bypassing the conscious mind, alter the scripts of your unconscious mind, and reach your superconscious mind.

Workshop B: How to Find the One You've Always Wanted

Learn the greatest secret of love. Discover why the heart of a woman is a man and the heart of a man is a woman.

Overcome the fear of love and intimacy. Engage in personal dialogues with your Saturn, the planet of avoidance and separation. Discovery how this planet holds the key to your unconscious assumptions that obstructs your relationships.

Discover those needs that are in harmony and those that are in conflict. Planetary chemistry produces the internal voices that show how these energies function in your life — how they can be sources of happiness or frustration in a relationship.

Understand the planetary chemistry of your friend or lover. This will open your eyes to a new way of looking at another person. Once you have understood how the planets work, no one will never be a mystery to you again.

FURTHER ADVENTURES WITH PLANETARY CHEMISTRY

Discover the kind of chemistry you need from other people to relate harmoniously with them. You will learn specific information that relates to your own planetary patterns. You will learn how to listen to the voices of these patterns and know what they mean.

Workshop C: One Day Workshop for Six Couples – Explore and Enhance Your Planetary Chemistry

This workshop is designed to help you and your mate discover what you are really like together. Separate planetary charts are drawn for both of you and then you will creatively compare them using unusual methods for awakening insights. Let the planets show you the way. Share in the discovery of how to live a more loving and creative intimacy.

- What do we really need from each other?
- How can we help each other be more successful?
- What are our potentials for spiritual growth?
- What are our primary conflicts and frustrations and how can we free ourselves from them?
- What are the missing parts within each of us that we can help awaken?
- How can we find a sense of self-worth and feel that we are truly loving?
- When is the right time to put our plans into action?
- What is happening in our life now and what can we do to cooperate with the events creatively?

If you would like, more time can be spent on one category. Each one-day workshop for six couples is very special because it is created out of the uniqueness of your relationship together and is adapted to your own particular needs.

Workshop D: Do You Really Understand Your Child?

Do you wonder how to inspire your child's growth? Have you been blaming yourself without reason? In this workshop, you will discover how your child relates to life and to you. The secret is in the planets for they reveal the special skills, talents, and attitudes that your child inherited from his past. This workshop will help you to explore these planets and discover the unique chemistry between you and your child.

Workshop E: Three Hour Workshop for You Alone

We can choose any of the areas you want to work on and the material you would like to cover. You can awaken some very important personal insights through the positive intensity of this solo journey

Workshop F: How to Use the Planets For Every Day of Your Life

How many times have you asked "What is going on?" What is happening to me?" and have not come up with any satisfying answer. No need to wonder any longer. When you take this one-day workshop you will learn how to answer all these questions and understand where you are going or what's happening to you. You will even be able to plot your own planetary weather months in advance. This is a great adventure.

OTHER SERVICES
(The following services are $75.00 each)

Personal Planetary Profiles

A thorough analysis of your life is made with you and recorded on tape in a personal session or on the phone from any place in the world.

Insights For Therapists

If you are a therapist and would like a refreshing view of how to help others, maybe you need just a few insights to trigger a new level of understanding or find out what areas are your greatest assets. Your own planetary patterns will point the way for you as well as for your clients.

Enhance Your Spiritual Practices

Whatever spiritual disciplines you practice, you can do them much better if you know your talents or assumed limitations. These areas are clearly drawn by the planetary patterns that were formed at the moment of your birth. My own experience as a Yoga monk of eleven years has given me great sympathy for the struggles of spiritual life. Let your planets guide you in your best direction.

Planetary Journeys for Musicians and Other Artists

If you feel blocked or unable to turn on your creative switch, you can access your unconscious and find your superconscious well of unlimited inspiration. Find new sounds and new colors. This is a journey well worth taking because you can tap the creative power of the planets at the right moment. Learn to create when your planetary energies are supporting you — avoid those times when they fail you — when nothing works out. Specific time and dates for best results can be given and a creative schedule can be planned.

Business Plans and Career Moves

If you are thinking of going into business or changing your job, you need a plan to know when and what to do. Avoid spinning your wheels or wasting your energy. Timing is everything. Let the planets show you the way. Learn to act when the planetary energies are moving your way.

Helpful Solutions for Everyday Problems

In any moment when you have an urgent question, the answer is also contained in that moment. If we do an analysis of the planetary conditions that prevail at the time you have a question, we can find the answer to that question. This is not something that needs to be believed. It is simply experienced as a reality. Strangely enough, this kind of analysis transcends time, because the motion of the planets mirror coming events.

Prints of the cover art and other works by Christa Marshall can be obtained by contacting her at:

P.O. Box 170097
San Francisco, California 94117.

FURTHER ADVENTURES WITH PLANETARY CHEMISTRY

ORDER FORM   (Please make a copy to use.)

☐ A. Enclosed is $3.00 and a self-addressed, stamped envelope for the computer readout of my planetary birth patterns which I wish to translate by using this book.

    ☐ I am also sending $3.00 for another person's birth patterns. All birth information is filled in below. (If time unknown, we will use sunrise.)

☐ B. Enclosed is $6.00 and a self-addressed, stamped envelope for the computer readout of my planetary birth patterns with translation of symbols and energy fields.

    ☐ I am also sending $6.00 for another person's birth patterns with translation of symbols and energy fields. All birth information is filled in below. (If time unknown, we will use sunrise.)

☐ C. I wish to have a comparison made between me and my _____ . Enclosed please find $30 and a self-addressed, stamped envelope. All birth information is filled in below. (If time unknown, we will use sunrise.)

☐ D. I would like to receive the following service listed under Other Services:_____ . Enclosed is my check for $75, birth data, and address. (Appointments may be arranged by phone or in person.)

☐ E. Please send a copy of this book as a gift from me to:

Name_____ Address _____

City _____ State _____ Zip _____

My check for $17.95 ($14.95 plus $3.00 for shipping) is enclosed. (If California resident, please add $1.16 sales tax.)

BIRTH DATA

Name_____ Address _____

City _____ State _____ Zip _____

Date of Birth _____ Time _____ Place _____

Second Name _____

Date of Birth _____ Time _____ Place _____

      (Example: 10/11/65, 4:00 pm, Racine, WI)

Send all orders to **Amrita Publications, P.O. Box 2008, San Anselmo, California 94979.**